Other Books by
Mary Hollingsworth

A Few Hallelujahs for Your Ho Hums
Apple Blossoms
The Divorce Recovery Guide
Fireside Stories of Love, Life, and Laughter
For Mom with Love
The Grief Adjustment Guide
Help! I Need a Bulletin Board
Hugs for Women
It's a One-derful Life!
Just Between Friends
Living Lights, Shining Stars
On Raising Children
Rainbows
Speaking of Love
Together Forever

and more than fifty books for children,
including these:

My Little Bible
The International Children's Story Bible
Just Imagine with Barney the Dinosaur
The Kids-Life Bible Storybook
Hugs for Kids

FIRESIDE STORIES

of Faith, Family, and Friendship

WRITTEN AND COMPILED BY

MARY HOLLINGSWORTH

WORD PUBLISHING
NASHVILLE
A Thomas Nelson Company

FIRESIDE STORIES OF FAITH, FAMILY, AND FRIENDSHIP
Copyright © 2000 by Mary Hollingsworth, Shady Oaks Studio, Bedford, Texas.

Published by Word Publishing, a unit of Thomas Nelson Publishers,
P.O. Box 141000, Nashville, Tennessee 37214. All rights reserved.

Unless otherwise indicated, Scripture quotations used in this book are from the
Holy Bible, New International Version (NIV). Copyright © 1973, 1978, 1984,
International Bible Society. Used by permission of Zondervan Bible Publishers.

Scripture references marked NCV are from the Holy Bible, New Century Version,
copyright © 1987, 1988, 1991 by Word Publishing. All rights reserved.

Research Associates: Vicki Graham and Rhonda Hogan

Unless otherwise attributed, entries are by the author.

Library of Congress Cataloging-in-Publication Data

Hollingsworth, Mary, 1947–
    Fireside stories of faith, family, and friendship / written and compiled by Mary
Hollingsworth.
       p. cm.
    Includes bibliographical references.
    ISBN 0-8499-4264-0 (trade paper)
    1. Christian life—Anecdotes. I. Title.
BV4517 .H64 2001
242—dc21   00–047704

Printed in the United States of America
00 01 02 03 04 05 06 07 08 09 PHX 9 8 7 6 5 4 3 2 1

*T*o the ones I love:
my family,
my friends,
and God—
my favorite Author and
the Perfecter of my faith

Contents

CONTENTS

Preface

*F*aith, *Family, and Friendship.* How can one puny writer presume to write about all three of these amazing topics in one book? Each topic could fill volumes and, indeed, libraries on its own.

Still, in my own life, these three are so vital and intertwined that I can't imagine how someone could separate them. I learned faith from my family and through my friendships. My faith draws me ever closer to my friends and family because we all share the same God and Lord. My friends are my family, and my family members are my friends. And faith is the glue that holds my family and friendships together. They are, in my mind, inseparable.

Like you, I have friends and family on many different levels. Some are close, intimate friends and family with whom I share secrets and feelings of complete trust and emotional safety. Others are business and professional friends that have developed over the years. Still others are church friends I see weekly or family members I see only rarely. Each of these holds a special place of honor in my life.

The stories in this collection look at family, friendship, and faith from various viewpoints. Some are funny; some are sad. Some are long; some are short. Some leave you pondering life; others leave you contented and fulfilled.

I wish I could take credit for all the stories in this book. I'd have loved writing these delightful tales. Alas! Others, better writers than I, deserve the credit for most of them, and I gratefully acknowledge their work.

I pray that these wonderful stories will touch your life with meaning. Perhaps one will bring you closer to a distant friend, an alienated family member, or even more important, your forsaken God. And if it does, my work will have all been worth it.

Mary Hollingsworth

Acknowledgments

$\mathcal{H}$eartfelt *thanks to my friends and family at Word Publishing,* who dedicate themselves to the wonderful work of taking words of faith, hope, and salvation to the world. Your calling is noble, your task is daunting, and your reward will be great. Thank you, each of you, for your faithfulness in all you do.

Humble thanks to the authors whose writings are included here. This book would be so much less without you.

And thanks to these other friends, without whom I could not have completed this joyful task: Vicki Graham, Charlotte Greeson, Rhonda Hogan, Nancy Norris, and Doris Williams. Blessings and joy!

I love to tell the story!
'Twill be my theme in glory—
To tell the old, old story
Of Jesus and His love.

———

Catherine Hankey

Before You Ask

One night I had worked hard to help a mother in the labor ward but, in spite of all we could do, she died, leaving us with a tiny, premature baby and a crying two-year-old daughter. We would have difficulty keeping the baby alive as we had no incubator (since we had no electricity) and no special feeding facilities. Although we lived on the equator, nights were often chilly with treacherous drafts. One student midwife went to get the box we had for such babies and the cotton wool in which the baby would be wrapped.

Another student went to stoke up the fire and fill a hot-water bottle. She came back shortly in distress to tell me that in filling the bottle it had burst. Rubber perishes easily in tropical climates. "And it is our last water bottle!" she exclaimed.

As in the West, it is no good crying over spilt milk, so in Central Africa it might be considered no good crying over burst water bottles. They do not grow on trees, and there are no drugstores down forest pathways.

"All right," I said, "put the baby as near the fire as you

1

safely can, and sleep between the baby and the door to keep it free from drafts. Your job is to keep the baby warm."

The following noon, as I did most days, I went to have prayers with the orphanage children. I gave the youngsters various suggestions of things to pray about and told them about the tiny baby. I explained our problem about keeping the baby warm enough, mentioning the hot-water bottle. The baby so easily could die if it got chills. I also told them of the two-year-old sister, crying because her mother had died.

During the prayer time, one ten-year-old girl, Ruth, prayed the usual blunt prayer of our African children. "Please, God," she prayed, "send us a water bottle. It'll be no good tomorrow, God, as the baby will be dead, so please send it this afternoon."

While I gasped inwardly at the audacity of the prayer, she added by way of corollary, "And while You're about it, would You please send a dolly for the little girl so she'll know You really love her?"

As often with children's prayers, I was put on the spot. Could I honestly say, "Amen"? I just did not believe that God could do this. Oh, yes, I know that He can do everything. The Bible says so. But there are limits, aren't there? The only way God could answer this particular prayer would be by sending me a parcel from the homeland. I had been in Africa for almost four years and had never, ever received a parcel from home. Anyway, if anyone did send me a parcel, who would put in a hot-water bottle? I lived on the equator!

Halfway through the afternoon, while I was teaching in the nurses' training school, a message was sent that there was a car at my front door. By the time I reached home, the car had gone, but there, on the verandah, was a large, twenty-two pound parcel. I felt tears pricking my eyes. I could not open the parcel alone, so I sent for the orphanage children.

Together we pulled off the string, carefully undoing each knot. We folded the paper, taking care not to tear it unduly. Excitement was mounting. Some thirty or forty pairs of eyes were focused on the large cardboard box.

From the top I lifted out brightly colored, knitted jerseys. Eyes sparkled as I gave them out. Then there were the knitted bandages for the leprosy patients, and the children looked a little bored. Then came a box of mixed raisins and sultanas that would make a nice batch of buns for the weekend. Then, as I put my hand in again, I felt the—could it really be? I grasped it and pulled it out. Yes, a brand-new, rubber, hot-water bottle! I cried. I had not asked God to send it; I had not truly believed that He could.

Ruth was in the front row of the children. She rushed forward, crying out, "If God has sent the bottle, He must have sent the dolly, too!" Rummaging down to the bottom of the box, she pulled out the small, beautifully dressed dolly. Her eyes shone! She had never doubted. Looking up at me, she asked, "Can I go over with you, Mummy, and give this dolly to that little girl so she'll know that Jesus really loves her?"

The parcel had been on the way for five whole months!

Packed up by former Sunday school class members whose leader had heard and obeyed God's prompting to send a hot-water bottle, even to the equator. And one of the girls had put in a dolly for an African child . . . *five months before* in answer to the believing prayer of a ten-year-old girl to bring it "that afternoon."

"Before they call I will answer"! (Isaiah 65:24)

———

Helen Roseveare
medical missionary from England to Zaire, Africa

Look Up Here!

M any years ago I used to call on a man in the Veterans'
Hospital. He had suffered a series of heart attacks and had
undergone major surgery. During his rehabilitation he stayed
at the Veterans' Hospital.

One day when I arrived to visit, I saw a touching scene.
This man had a young son, and during his confinement in
the hospital, he had made a little wooden truck for his boy.
Since the boy was not allowed to go into the ward and visit
his father, an orderly had brought the gift down to the child,
who was waiting in front of the hospital with his mother.
The father was looking out of a fifth-floor window, watching his son unwrap the gift.

The little boy opened the package, and his eyes widened
when he saw that wonderful little truck. He hugged it to his
chest.

Meanwhile, the father was walking back and forth behind
the windowpane trying to get his son's attention.

The little boy put the truck down and reached up and
hugged the orderly and thanked him for the truck. And all

the while the frustrated father was going through dramatic gestures, trying to say, "It's me, son. I made that truck for you. I gave that to you. Look up here!" I could almost read his lips.

Finally the mother and the orderly turned the boy's attention up to that fifth-floor window. And then the boy cried, "Daddy! Oh, thank you! I miss you, Daddy! Come home, Daddy. Thank you for my truck."

And the father stood in the window with tears pouring down his cheeks.

How much like that child we are. We are shut away in our caves of loneliness and discouragement, and then God brings along the gifts of rest and refreshment, wise counsel, close, personal friends. And we fall in love with the gifts, rather than the Giver!

He gives us a verse of Scripture, and we worship the Bible rather than the One that gave it. He gives us a loving wife or husband or friend, and we fall in love with the person rather than the One who gave us that important individual. He gives us a good job, and we love the job more than we love Him. And all the while He stands at the window and says, "Look up here. I gave that to you." He longs to have us look up and say, "Oh, thank You, Father! I miss You. I want to be with You."

———

Charles R. Swindoll
Elijah: A Man of Heroism and Humility

The Twenty-third Psalm ... Almost

Now that many years have passed since my delightful mother-in-law was called to that large mothers-in-law's meeting in the sky, I am often still to be found smiling at her remarks. She had a wonderful habit of getting expressions just slightly wrong, such as, "Making money while the hay shines."

I remember once in church hearing her intoning, with very serious face, the words of the twenty-third psalm: "He maketh me to lie down in green waters."

Nigel Rees

The Funeral Procession

A woman was leaving a 7-Eleven store with her morning coffee when she noticed a most unusual funeral procession approaching the nearby cemetery. A long black hearse was followed by a second long black hearse about fifty feet behind. Behind the second hearse was a solitary woman walking a pit bull on a leash. Behind her were two hundred women walking in single file.

The woman couldn't stand the curiosity, so she respectfully approached the woman walking with the dog and said, "I am so sorry for your loss, and I know now is a bad time to disturb you, but I've never seen a funeral like this. Whose is it?"

The woman replied, "Well, in that first hearse is my husband."

"What happened to him?" she asked.

"My dog attacked and killed him."

"Well, who is in the second hearse?"

"My mother-in-law. She was trying to help my husband when the dog turned on her."

A poignant and thoughtful moment of silence passed between the two women.

"Could I borrow that dog?" asked the first woman.

"Get in line."

———

Originator Unknown

Seeing Out

✝

*I*n the early part of 1997, a woman in our city was given a terminal diagnosis by her doctor. Now, the woman had a horrible fear of being buried in the dark ground; so she came to our funeral home to make her own alternate final arrangements.

As we helped her make final choices and special plans, she requested two very unusual things. First, she wanted me to find a glass-topped casket for her. I explained that the full-couch, glass caskets are no longer made, but she insisted that I try to locate one. So, after extensive searching, I finally found one casket that met her criteria and had it shipped to us, at great expense.

Next, she said she wanted to buy a space in our mausoleum . . . but not just *any* space. She wanted a space on the top row. *Well, okay, that's fine,* I was thinking. Then she explained why. She wanted to have the top space so she could have a skylight installed in it. That way, with a glass-topped casket and a skylight . . . she could *see out.*

When the woman died later that spring, her family followed her written instructions to the letter. At major expense, we had the skylight installed in our mausoleum, and she was placed in her glass-top casket into the space. And there she lies today happily *looking out at eternity.*

———

Lee Nelson
funeral director

No Worries

$\mathcal{A}$ 102-year-old woman was asked whether she still had any worries at her advanced age.

"No, I haven't," she replied.

"And to what do you attribute your peace of mind?" she was asked.

"Everything's been fine since my youngest son went into an old folks' home."

———

Nigel Rees

A Goldie Oldie

*S*aturday mornings were one of my favorite times of the week. My mother-in-law and I drove from our Kansas farm into the small town nearby to do our weekly errands—go to the grocery store, take clothes to the cleaners, go to the post office, and other chores. But the best part, believe it or not, was our weekly visit to the nursing home in town. We went to see Aunt Goldie.

At the age of 102, Aunt Goldie was a feisty, mentally bright, and delightful little lady. When she turned 100, the nursing home had given Aunt Goldie a grand centennial birthday party. We had all dressed up and driven into town for the gala. The 102-year-old honoree happily donned her bright red dress and proceeded to do the Charleston with my husband, who was then half her age. It was a fun evening!

From time to time I would take my guitar with me for our visit. Aunt Goldie loved music. So, I would sit in her room and sing folk songs for her. She would tap her foot and clap her hands to the music, laughing and singing along. Her nursing home friends and neighbors would come and stand in the door or roll their wheelchairs down the hall and sit outside her room, enjoying the music. It was always a happy experience for me.

Most Saturdays, when Aunt Goldie felt like getting out, we would say, "Aunt Goldie, where would you like to go today?"

Her answer was always the same: "Can we go to the A&W root beer place? I'd sure like to have a hot dog and a frosted-mug root beer."

And off we'd go to have lunch at the A&W. She always looked forward to it, because the food at the nursing home tended to be bland and boring.

Aunt Goldie was a happy soul, for the most part. But one thing made her a little melancholy—talking about her family and friends. At that point in her long life, Aunt Goldie had outlived almost everyone she knew. Her parents had been gone for decades. Her husband had been dead for many years. She had outlived her children and even some of her grandchildren. Her aunts, uncles, and cousins had gone on ahead of her. All of her friends were gone too. Except for a few of us in her extended family, she was alone in the world.

She would pat herself on the chest and then point toward heaven and say, "I'm ready to go. I'm ready to go." And she would smile the contented smile of the faithful.

During her 102nd year, Aunt Goldie suffered a stroke. While the stroke did not damage her mind in any way, it left her unable to speak. The stroke came just one week before her death. Even then she continued to communicate with us by nodding and touching.

The day before she died, I went to see her. I sat by her bed and held her hand for a while. Then I pulled out my guitar and sang to her for about an hour. She smiled and clapped, even though she could no longer sing with me.

Before I left, I prayed with Aunt Goldie and gave her a hug. And I'll never forget the last thing she said to me, even though it wasn't spoken in words. She patted herself on the chest and pointed up toward heaven. Her message of faith and hope was clear.

There were twelve people at Aunt Goldie's funeral—everyone she had left in the world was there. And it dawned on me that there comes a time when dying is more inviting than living, because you eventually have more friends and family on the other side of the eternal door than on this side. So, the thought of walking through that door is a happy one. And I smiled as I remembered Aunt Goldie's final message to me. She was, indeed, ready to go. And, oh! What a reunion she must have had.

Bearly a Christian

*A*n atheist was taking a walk through the woods, admiring all that the "accident of evolution" had created.

What majestic trees! What powerful rivers! What beautiful animals! he said to himself. As he walked alongside the river, he heard a rustling in the bushes behind him. As he turned to look, he saw a seven-foot grizzly bear charge toward him.

He ran as fast as he could up the path. He looked over his shoulder and saw that the bear was closing in on him. He tried to run even faster, so scared that tears were coming to his eyes. He looked over his shoulder again, and the bear was even closer. His heart was pumping frantically as he tried to run even faster, but he tripped and fell on the ground. He rolled over to pick himself up and saw the bear right on top of him raising his paw to kill him. At that instant he cried out, "Oh God, help me!"

Just then, time stopped. The bear froze; the forest was silent; the river even stopped moving. A bright light shone upon the man, and a voice came out of the sky, saying, "You deny my existence all of these years, teach others I don't exist, even credit my creation to a cosmic accident, and now do you expect me to help you out of this predicament? Am I to count you as a believer?"

The atheist, ever so proud, looked into the light and said, "It would be rather hypocritical to ask to be a Christian after all these years, but could you make the bear a Christian?"

"Very well," said the voice.

As the light went out, the river ran, and the sounds of the forest continued, the bear put his paw down. The bear then brought both paws together, bowed his head, and said: "Lord, I thank you for this food, which I am about to receive."

———

Originator Unknown

Twinkies and Root Beer

There once was a little boy who wanted to meet God. He knew it was a long trip to where God lived, so he packed his Twinkies and a six-pack of root beer, and he started on his journey. When he had gone about three blocks, he met an old man. He was sitting in a park, staring at some pigeons.

The boy sat down next to him and opened his suitcase. He was about to take a drink from his root beer when he noticed that the old man looked hungry, so he offered him a Twinkie. The old man gratefully accepted it and smiled at him. His smile was so pretty that the boy wanted to see it again, so he offered him a root beer. Once again, the man smiled at him.

The boy was delighted. They sat there all afternoon eating, drinking root beer, and smiling, yet they never said a word. As it grew dark, the boy realized how tired he was, and he got up to leave. Before he had gone more than a few steps, he turned around, ran back to the old man, and gave him a hug. The man gave the boy his biggest smile ever.

When the boy opened the door to his own home a short

time later, his mother was surprised by the look of joy on his face. She asked him, "What did you do today that makes you so happy?"

He replied, "I had lunch with God."

But before his mother could respond, he added, "You know what? He's got the most beautiful smile I've ever seen!"

Meanwhile, the old man, also radiant with joy, returned to his home. His neighbor was stunned by the look of peace on his face, and she asked, "What did you do today that made you so happy?"

He replied, "I ate Twinkies in the park with God." But before his neighbor could respond, he added, "You know, he's much younger than I expected!"

———

Originator Unknown

Faith

Faith is a prism,
refracting the cheerful light of God
into vibrant colors
and scattering them into
the mundane corners of life.

Mary Hollingsworth
A Few Hallelujahs for Your Ho Hums

Precious Lord

$\mathcal{B}$ack in 1932, I was thirty-two years old and a fairly new husband. My wife, Nettie, and I were living in a little apartment on Chicago's south side.

One hot August afternoon I had to go to St. Louis, where I was to be the featured soloist at a large Christian meeting. I didn't want to go. Nettie was in the last month of pregnancy with our first child. But a lot of people were expecting me in St. Louis. So I kissed Nettie good-bye, clattered downstairs to our Model A and, in a fresh Lake Michigan breeze, chugged out of Chicago on Route 66. However, outside the city, I discovered that in my anxiety about leaving, I had forgotten my music case. I wheeled around and headed back.

I found Nettie sleeping peacefully. I hesitated by her bed; something was strongly telling me to stay. But eager to get on my way, and not wanting to disturb Nettie, I shrugged off the feeling and quietly slipped out of the room with my music.

The next night, in the steaming St. Louis heat, the crowd

called out for me to sing again and again. When I finally sat down, a messenger boy ran up with a Western Union telegram. I ripped open the envelope. Pasted on the yellow sheet were the horrible words: YOUR WIFE JUST DIED.

People were happily singing and clapping around me, but I could hardly keep from crying out. I rushed to a phone and called home. All I could hear on the other end was, "Nettie is dead. Nettie is dead." When I got back, I learned that Nettie had given birth to a boy. I swung between grief and joy. Yet that night, the baby died too. I buried Nettie and our little boy together, in the same casket. Then I fell apart.

For days I closeted myself. I felt that God had done me an injustice. I didn't want to serve Him anymore or write gospel songs. I just wanted to go back to that jazz world I once knew so well. But then, as I hunched alone in that dark apartment those first sad days, I thought back to the afternoon I went to St. Louis. Something kept telling me to stay with Nettie. Was that something God? Oh, if I had paid more attention to Him that day, I would have stayed and been with Nettie when she died.

From that moment on I vowed to listen more closely to Him. But still I was lost in grief. Everyone was kind to me, especially a friend, Professor Fry, who seemed to know what I needed.

On the following Saturday evening he took me up to Malone's Poro College, a neighborhood music school. It was quiet; the late evening sun crept through the curtained windows. I sat down at the piano, and my hands began to browse over the keys. Something happened to me then. I felt at peace. I felt as though I could reach out and touch God. I found myself playing a melody, and the words just seemed to fall into place:

Precious Lord, take my hand, lead me on,
   help me stand—
I am tired, I am weak, I am worn;
Thro' the storm, thro' the night, lead me
   on to the light—
Take my hand, precious Lord, lead me home.

As the Lord gave me these words and melody, He also healed my spirit. I learned that, when we are in our deepest grief, when we feel farthest from God, this is when He is closest and when we are most open to His restoring power. And so, I go on living for God willingly and joyfully, until that day comes when He will take me and gently lead me home.

———

Tommy A. Dorsey
Guideposts Magazine

Tommy

Some twelve years ago, I stood watching my university students file into the classroom for our first session in Theology of Faith. That was the day I first saw Tommy. My eyes and my mind both blinked. He was combing his long, flaxen hair, which hung six inches below his shoulders. It was the first time I had ever seen a boy with hair that long. I guess it was just coming into fashion then. I know, in my mind, that it isn't what's *on* your head but what's *in* it that counts, but on that day I was unprepared, and my emotions flipped. I immediately filed Tommy under "s" for strange—very strange.

Tommy turned out to be the "atheist in residence" in my Theology of Faith course. He constantly objected to, smirked at, or whined about the possibility of an unconditionally loving Father-God. We lived with each other in relative peace for one semester, although I admit he was, for me, at times, a serious pain in the back pew.

When he came up at the end of the course to turn in his final exam, he asked in a slightly cynical tone, "Do you think I'll ever find God?"

I decided instantly on a little shock therapy. "No!" I said very emphatically.

"Oh," he responded, "I thought that was the product you were pushing."

I let him get five steps from the classroom door and then called out, "Tommy! I don't think you'll ever find Him, but I am absolutely certain that He will find you."

He shrugged a little and left my class and my life. I felt slightly disappointed at the thought that he had missed my clever line "He will find you." At least I thought it was clever.

Later I heard that Tommy had graduated, and I was duly grateful. Then came a sad report. I heard that Tommy had terminal cancer. Before I could search him out, he came to see me. When he walked into my office, his body was very badly wasted, and the long hair had all fallen out as a result of chemotherapy. But his eyes were bright and his voice was firm for the first time, I believe.

"Tommy, I've thought about you so often. I hear you are sick," I blurted out.

"Oh yes, very sick. I have cancer in both lungs. It's a matter of weeks."

"Can you talk about it, Tom?"

"Sure. What would you like to know?"

"What's it like to be only twenty-four and dying?"

"Well, it could be worse."

"Like what?" I asked.

"Well, like being fifty and having no values or ideals, like being fifty and thinking that booze, seducing women, and making money are the real 'biggies' in life."

I began to look through my mental file cabinet under "s" where I had filed Tommy as strange. (It seems as though everybody I try to reject by classification God sends back into my life to educate me.)

"But what I really came to see you about," Tom said, "is something you said to me on the last day of class." (He remembered.) He continued, "I asked you if you thought I would ever find God, and you said, 'No!' which surprised me. Then you said, 'But He will find you.' I thought about that a lot, even though my search for God was hardly intense at that time." (My *clever* line. He had thought about that a lot!)

"But when the doctors removed a lump from my groin and told me that it was malignant, then I got serious about locating God. And when the malignancy spread into my vital organs, I really began banging bloody fists against the bronze doors of heaven. But God did not come out. In fact, nothing happened.

"Did you ever try anything for a long time with great effort and with no success? You get psychologically glutted, fed up with trying. And then you quit. Well, one day I woke up, and instead of throwing a few more futile appeals over that high brick wall to a God who may be or may not be there, I just quit. I decided that I didn't really care about God, about an afterlife, or anything like that.

"I decided to spend what time I had left doing something more profitable. I thought about you and your class, and I remembered something else you had said: 'The essential sadness is to go through life without loving. But it would be almost equally sad to go through life and leave this world without ever telling those you loved that you had loved them.'

"So I began with the hardest one—my dad. He was reading the newspaper when I approached him.

"I said, 'Dad?'

"'Yes, what?' he asked without lowering the newspaper.

"'Dad, I would like to talk with you.'

"'Well, talk.'

"'I mean . . . it's really important.'

"The newspaper came down three slow inches. 'What is it?'

"'Dad, I love you. I just wanted you to know that.'"

Tom smiled at me and said with obvious satisfaction, as though he felt a warm and secret joy flowing inside of him, "The newspaper fluttered to the floor. Then my father did two things I could never remember him ever doing before. He cried, and he hugged me. And we talked all night, even though he had to go to work the next morning. It felt so good to be close to my father, to see his tears, to feel his hug, to hear him say that he loved me, too.

"It was easier with my mother and little brother. They cried with me, too, and we hugged each other and started saying really nice things to each other. We shared the things we had been keeping secret for so many years.

"I was only sorry about one thing: that I had waited so long. Here I was just beginning to open up to all the people I had actually been close to, and I was dying.

"Then one day I turned around, and God was there. He didn't come to me when I pleaded with Him. I guess I was like an animal trainer holding out a hoop: 'C'mon, jump through. C'mon, I'll give you three days, three weeks.' Apparently God does things in His own way and at His own hour. But the important thing is that He was there. He found me. You were right. He found me even after I had stopped looking for Him."

"Tommy," I practically gasped, "I think you are saying something very important and much more universal than you realize. To me, at least, you are saying that the surest way to find God is not to make Him a private possession, a problem solver, or an instant consolation in time of need, but rather by opening to love. You know, the apostle John said that. He said, 'God is love, and anyone who lives in love is living with God, and God is living in him.'

"Tom, could I ask you a favor? You know, when I had you in class, you were a real pain. But (laughing) you can make it all up to me now. Would you come into my present Theology of Faith course and tell them what you have just told me? If I told them the same thing, it wouldn't be half as effective as if you were to tell them."

"Ooooh . . . I was ready for you, Professor, but I don't know if I'm ready for your class."

"Tom, think about it. If and when you *are* ready, give me a call."

In a few days Tommy called and said he was ready for the class and that he wanted to do that for God and for me. So we scheduled a date. However, Tommy never made it. He had another appointment, far more important than the one with my class and me.

Of course, Tommy's life was not really ended by his death; it was only changed. He made the great step from faith into vision. He found a life far more beautiful than the eye of man has ever seen or the ear of man has ever heard or the mind of man has ever imagined.

Before he died, we talked one last time.

"I'm not going to make it to your class," he said.

"I know, Tom."

"Will you tell them for me? Will you tell the whole world for me?"

"I will, Tom. I'll tell them. I'll do my best."

So, to all of you who have been kind enough to hear this simple statement about love, thank you for listening. And to you, Tommy, somewhere in the sunlit, verdant hills of heaven: I told them, Tommy . . . as best I could.

———

John Powell
Professor, Loyola University

Who Are You?

$\mathcal{A}$ young woman teacher with obvious liberal tendencies explained to her class of small children that she was an atheist. She asked her class if they were atheists too. Not really knowing what atheism was, but wanting to be like their teacher, their tiny hands exploded into the air like fleshy fireworks.

There was, however, one exception. A beautiful little girl named Lucy did not go along with the crowd. The teacher asked her why she had decided to be different.

"Because I'm not an atheist," she said.

Then asked the teacher, "What are you?"

"I'm a Christian."

The teacher was a little perturbed by then, and her face was slightly red. She asked Lucy why she was a Christian.

"Well, I was brought up knowing and loving Jesus. My mom is a Christian, and my dad is a Christian, so I am a Christian."

The teacher was now angry. "That's no reason," she said loudly. "What if your mom was a moron, and your dad was a moron. What would you be then?" She paused and smiled because she just knew she *had* the little girl.

"Then," answered Lucy, "I'd be an atheist!"

———

Originator Unknown

Confidence

꙼

$\mathcal{F}$aith is a living, daring
confidence in God's grace,
so sure and certain
that a man could stake his life on it
a thousand times.

———

Martin Luther

God's Little Workshop

There was a small sign over the door that read "God's Little Workshop." It was the laboratory of Dr. George Washington Carver, and he proved its truth throughout his brilliant life.

The story goes that Dr. Carver once held a simple peanut in his hand and asked God to tell him its secret. Then, as if God had actually spoken to him, Dr. Carver suddenly remembered the three scientific laws that had already come from God—the principles of temperature, pressure, and compatibility.

At that point, and trusting God's lead, Dr. Carver began uncovering the incredible wealth of the tiny peanut. He discovered such properties as proteins, oils, cellulose, pigments, and carbohydrates. Then, putting these properties to work, he created over three hundred products from the peanut, including dyes, stains, soaps, rubber, beverages, shoe polish, milk, leathers, and explosives.

God took a slave boy, who had once been swapped for a racehorse, and led him to be one of the world's greatest scientists. He was able to do it because God's great servant believed that his laboratory was God's little workshop, not his own.

So, the next time you feel as if you're only "working for peanuts," think of Dr. Carver and the vast wealth he discovered in one of God's tiny creations. Then turn *your* life into God's little workshop and see what amazing things he can do through you.

———

Mary Hollingsworth
A Few Hallelujahs for Your Ho Hums

The Tablecloth

The brand-new minister and his wife, newly assigned to reopen a church in suburban Brooklyn, arrived in early October excited about their opportunities. When they saw the church building, it was very run-down and needed much work.

They set a goal to have everything done in time to have their first service on Christmas Eve. They worked hard, repairing pews, plastering walls, and painting, and on December 18 they were ahead of schedule and almost finished.

On December 19 a terrible tempest—a driving rain-storm—hit the area and lasted for two days. On the twenty-first, the minister went over to the church. His heart sank when he saw that the roof had leaked, causing a large area of plaster about twenty feet high by eight feet wide to fall off the front wall just behind the pulpit, beginning about head high.

The minister cleaned up the mess on the floor, and not knowing what else to do but postpone the Christmas Eve service, headed home. On the way he noticed that a local business was having a flea market sale for charity; so he stopped in.

One of the items for sale was a beautiful, handmade, ivory-colored, crocheted tablecloth with exquisite work, fine colors, and the Cross embroidered right in the center. It was just the right size to cover up the hole in the front wall. He bought it and headed back to the church.

By this time it had started to snow. An older woman, running from the opposite direction, was trying to catch the bus. She missed it. So the minister invited her to wait in the warm church for the next bus forty-five minutes later.

She sat in a pew and paid no attention to the minister while he got a ladder and hangers to put up the tablecloth as a wall tapestry. The minister could hardly believe how beautiful it looked, and it covered up the entire problem area.

Then he noticed the woman walking down the center aisle. Her face was pale white like a sheet.

"Sir," she asked, "where did you get that tablecloth?"

The minister explained. Then the woman asked him to check the lower right corner to see if the initials EBG were crocheted into it there. They were. They were the initials of the woman who had made that tablecloth thirty-five years before in Austria.

The stunned woman explained to the minister that before the war she and her husband were well-to-do people in Austria. When the Nazis came, she was forced to leave. Her husband was going to follow her the next week. She was captured, sent to prison, and never saw her husband or her home again.

The minister wanted to give her the tablecloth, but she made him keep it for the church. The minister insisted on driving her home; that was the least he felt he could do. She lived on the other side of Staten Island and was only in Brooklyn for the day for a housecleaning job.

What a wonderful service they had in the renovated church on Christmas Eve. The church was almost full. The music and the spirit were great.

At the end of the service, the minister and his wife greeted everyone at the door, and many said they would return. One older man, whom the minister recognized from the neighborhood, continued to sit in one of the pews and stare. The minister wondered why he wasn't leaving.

The man asked him where he had gotten the tablecloth on the front wall, because it was identical to one that his wife had made years ago when they lived in Austria before the war, and how could there be two tablecloths so much alike?

He told the minister how the Nazis came, how he forced his wife to flee for her safety, and he was supposed to follow her. But he was arrested and put in a prison. He never saw his wife or his home again all the thirty-five years in between.

The minister asked him if he would allow him to take him for a little ride. They drove to Staten Island to the same house where the minister had taken the woman three days earlier. He helped the man climb the three flights of stairs to the woman's apartment and he knocked on the door. There he witnessed the greatest Christmas reunion he could ever imagine.

———

A true story by Rob Reid

Missed Charity

✦

Outside the theater one night, the American actress Tallulah Bankhead encountered a group from the Salvation Army, tambourines as always well to the fore. She promptly dropped a fifty-dollar bill into one of the tambourines, saying, "Don't bother to thank me. I know what a perfectly ghastly season it's been for you Spanish dancers."

———

Dorothy Herrman

The Prank

I went to college at Abilene Christian University (ACU)—then a conservative, private school in West Texas. As college students are wont to do, we used practical jokes and pranks to overcome the stress of our studies and the boredom of a relatively small town. Some were better than others.

For instance, once we had a giant "flush out" to see what would happen if we flushed all the commodes in the whole dorm at one time. Stationing relay callers on each end of every floor, we had a simultaneous countdown: "Three! Two! One! Flush!"

Did you know that plumbing systems are not really built to have all the commodes in a dormitory for 318 girls flushed at one time? It is not—I repeat, *not*—recommended by the ACU administration and housing supervisor as an acceptable student activity.

Another student activity that is not recommended at ACU anymore is attempting to jump the twenty-five-foot-wide Gata fountain on a bicycle. Doctors and administrators

all agree that this particular activity is less than satisfactory
. . . never mind, healthy.

Still, one of my favorite pranks at ACU happened when I
was a freshman and living in Nelson Hall. Our dorm mother
was infamous for being extremely conservative and strict.
She is credited with saying that girls shouldn't wear patent-
leather shoes because the boys could see up their dresses.
She also said that girls shouldn't wear polka dots because
that made the boys want to poke them.

Another time, so it's said, she was walking behind a boy
and girl who were strolling across campus holding hands.
She rebuffed them for what she considered their inappropri-
ate physical contact by asking harshly, "Just what are you
saving for marriage?"

And the boy responded snidely, "The other hand!"

Anyway, the point is, she was not particularly broad-
minded about *anything* that did not appear completely pris-
tine and pure.

One evening the dorm mother left the dorm for an
evening out to dinner with friends. And you know what happens when the old cat's away. Two of the freshman girls,
looking for a way to break up the boredom, mixed up some
bright-red tempera paint in an old coffee can. Then they went
through the janitor's storage closets on each end of all three
floors of the dorm, opened the windows at the backs of the
closets, and reached outside with a long-handled paintbrush
to paint all the spotlights on the front of the dorm red.

None of us inside the dorm even knew anything had happened until the resident assistants on our floors came by to announce a dorm meeting in the parlor at 9:30 P.M. Wondering what this unusual, late-night meeting was about, all two hundred of us obediently trooped down to the parlor in our pajamas and fuzzy house shoes. It must have been the largest collection of weird hair curlers ever gathered in one place at one time. We looked like a convention of space freaks.

We sat in chairs, lounged on sofas, and stretched out on the floor all around the room. I ended up about five feet in front of where the dorm mother chose to stand for her big announcement. That proved to be a very poor choice.

When Old Stoneface came in, it was obvious from her countenance that she was not aglow with peace and joy from her evening out. Her stormy face caused a hush to fall across the gathering, and I scooted back about two feet to put a little more distance between her and me.

When everyone was quiet, she said coldly, "Girls, I called you to this meeting because something tragic has happened."

Naturally, we thought the president of the university had died or something. So, we sat up and listened in rapt attention as she went on.

"I went out to dinner tonight with some friends. But when I returned to the dorm, I was shocked—*horribly shocked!*—by what I saw."

We all looked at each other, puzzled. *What did she see?* we wondered.

"There, on the front of our dorm, I discovered six red spotlights!" (Muffled giggles from the back of the room.) "I was so ashamed." (More restrained giggles. We didn't dare laugh out loud.)

"Now, I fail to see anything funny about this situation. I have never been so embarrassed in my life." (The laughter died out.)

"Of course, I came inside and immediately called the security office. And when I told the chief of security that our dorm has red lights on the front, he said he'd be *right over.*"

That did it! All two hundred girls broke into wild laughter, including me. The harder we laughed, the angrier she became, and the harder we laughed. Finally, she turned on her heel and stomped out of the parlor and back to her apartment. She didn't speak to most of us for several days—a punishment we endured with joy, I might add.

Unfortunately, they discovered who the pranksters were, and the two girls were severely reprimanded and "campused" for the whole semester. The rest of us felt so sorry for them that we sneaked off-campus foods and treats (like pizza and Mac Eplan's pink cookies) to them in payment for the best laugh we'd ever had.

God's Perfection

$\mathcal{A}$t a fund-raising dinner for a Brooklyn school that caters to learning-disabled children, the father of one child was expected to give a speech extolling the dedicated staff's work. Instead, his opening remarks shocked the crowd of parents and teachers.

He cried out, "My son goes to this school, which teaches that everything God does is done with perfection. But where is the perfection in my son Shaya? My child cannot understand things as other children do. So tell me where is God's perfection?"

The audience, shocked by the man's anguished question, hushed. A few people coughed nervously as the father continued: "I believe that when God brings a child like this into the world, the perfection He seeks is in the way people react."

The father then told about the afternoon he and Shaya walked past a park where some boys Shaya knew were playing baseball.

"Do you think they will let me play?" Shaya asked.

The father knew that his son was not at all athletic and that most boys would not want him on their team. Nevertheless, Shaya's father understood that, if his son were to be chosen to play, it would give him a comfortable sense of belonging. So the father approached one of the boys in the field and asked if Shaya could play. The boy looked around for guidance from his teammates. Getting none, he took matters into his own hands.

"We're losing by six runs, and the game is in the eighth inning," he told the father. "I guess he can be on our team, and we'll try to put him up to bat in the ninth inning."

Shaya's father was ecstatic as Shaya smiled broadly. A team member told Shaya to put on a glove and go out to play short center field.

In the bottom of the eighth inning, Shaya's team scored a few runs but was still behind by three. In the bottom of the ninth inning, Shaya's team scored again. Now, with two outs and the bases loaded, and with the potential winning run on base, Shaya was up to bat.

Would the team actually take a chance on Shaya to bat home the winning run? the father wondered. Everyone knew it was all but impossible because Shaya didn't even know how to hold the bat properly, let alone hit with it.

Yet, as Shaya stepped up to the plate, the pitcher moved a few steps to lob the ball in softly so Shaya should at least be able to make contact. The first pitch came in, and Shaya swung clumsily and missed. One of Shaya's teammates came up behind Shaya and put his arms around him so together they could hold the bat and face the pitcher.

Again the pitcher took a few steps forward to toss the ball softly. As the pitch came in, Shaya and his teammate swung at the ball, and together they hit a slow ground ball. The pitcher picked up the soft grounder and could easily have thrown the ball to the first baseman. Shaya would have been out, and that would have ended the game. Instead, the pitcher took the ball and threw it on a high arc to right field, far beyond the reach of the first baseman.

Everyone started yelling, "Shaya, run to first! Run to first!"

Never in his life had Shaya run to first. So, now he scampered down the baseline, wide-eyed and startled. By the time he reached first base, the right fielder had the ball. He could have thrown the ball to the second baseman, who would tag out Shaya, still running. But the right fielder understood what the pitcher's intentions were; so he threw the ball high and far over the third baseman's head.

Everyone yelled, "Run to second! Run to second!"

Shaya ran toward second base as the runners ahead of him deliriously circled the bases toward home. Just as Shaya reached second base, the opposing shortstop ran to him, turned him in the direction of third base and shouted, "Run to third!"

As Shaya rounded third, the boys from both teams ran behind him screaming, "Shaya, run home!" Shaya ran home, stepped on home plate, and all eighteen boys lifted him on their shoulders. They made Shaya their hero, as he had just hit a grand slam and won the game for his team.

"That day," said the father softly, with tears now rolling down his face, "those eighteen boys reached their level of God's perfection."

———

Rabbi Paysach Krohn

I Took His Hand and Followed

*M*y dishes went unwashed today,
  I didn't make the bed.
I took his hand and followed
  where his eager footsteps led.

Oh, yes, we went adventuring,
  my little son and I . . .
Exploring all the great outdoors
  beneath the summer sky.

We waded in a crystal stream,
  we wandered through a wood . . .
My kitchen wasn't swept today,
  but life was rich and good.

We found a cool, sun-dappled glade,
  and now my small son knows
How mother bunny hides her nest,
  where Jack-in-the-pulpit grows.

We watched a robin feed her young,
   we climbed a sunlit hill . . .
Saw cloud-sheep scamper through the sky,
   we plucked a daffodil.

That my house was neglected,
   that I didn't brush the stairs,
In twenty years no one on earth
   will know or even care.

But that I've helped my little boy
   to noble manhood grow
In twenty years the whole wide world
   may look and see and know.

———

Author Unknown

Really Real

𝕎hat is *real?*" asked the Rabbit one day, when they were lying side by side near the nursery fender, before Nana came to tidy the room. "Does it mean having things that buzz inside you and a stick-out handle?"

"Real isn't how you are made," said the Skin Horse. "It's a thing that happens to you."

"Does it hurt?" asked the Rabbit.

"Sometimes," said the Skin Horse, for he was always truthful. "When you are Real, you don't mind being hurt."

"Does it happen all at once?" he asked.

"It doesn't happen all at once," said the Skin Horse. "You *become.* It takes a long time. That's why it doesn't often happen to people who break easily, or have sharp edges, or who have to be carefully kept. Generally, by the time you are Real, most of your hair has been loved off, and your eyes drop out, and you get loose in the joints and very shabby. But these things don't matter at all, because once you are Real you can't be ugly, except to people who don't understand."

———

Margery Williams
The Velveteen Rabbit

The trouble with cleaning the house
is that it gets dirty the next day anyway.
So, skip a week if you have to.
The children are the most
important thing.

Barbara Bush
former First Lady of the United States

Still Singing

You never know whose life you'll touch just by being yourself. When I was quite young, my father had one of the first telephones in our neighborhood. I remember well the polished old case fastened to the wall. The shiny receiver hung on the side of the box.

I was too little to reach the telephone, but I used to listen with fascination when my mother would talk to it. Then I discovered that somewhere inside the wonderful device lived an amazing person. Her name was "Information Please," and there was nothing she did not know. For instance, Information Please could supply anybody's number and the correct time.

My first personal experience with this genie in the bottle came one day while my mother was visiting a neighbor. Amusing myself at the tool bench in the basement, I whacked my finger with a hammer. The pain was terrible, but there didn't seem to be any reason for crying because there was no one home to give sympathy. I walked around the house sucking my throbbing finger, finally arriving at the stairway. The telephone! Quickly, I ran for the footstool in the parlor and dragged it to the landing. Climbing up, I unhooked the receiver and held it to my ear.

"Information Please," I said into the mouthpiece just above my head.

A click or two and a small, clear voice spoke into my ear: "Information."

"I hurt my finger!" I wailed into the phone. The tears came readily enough now that I had an audience.

"Isn't your mother home?" came the question.

"Nobody's home but me," I blubbered.

"Are you bleeding?" the voice asked.

"No," I replied. "I hit my finger with the hammer, and it hurts."

"Can you open your icebox?" she asked.

"Yes," I answered.

"Then chip off a little piece of ice and hold it to your finger," said the voice.

After that I called Information Please for everything. I asked her for help with my geography, and she told me where Philadelphia was. She helped me with my math. She told me my pet chipmunk, which I had caught in the park just the day before, would eat fruit and nuts.

Then there was the time Petey, our pet canary, died. I called Information Please and told her the sad story. She listened; then she said the usual things grownups say to soothe a child. But I was unconsoled.

I asked her, "Why is it that birds should sing so beautifully and bring joy to all families only to end up as a heap of feathers on the bottom of a cage?"

She must have sensed my deep concern, for she said quietly, "Paul, always remember that there are other worlds to sing in."

Somehow I felt better.

Another day I was on the telephone: "Information Please."

"Information," said the now familiar voice.

"How do you spell 'fix'?" I asked.

All this took place in a small town in the Pacific Northwest. When I was nine years old, we moved across the country to Boston. I missed my friend Information Please very much. She belonged in that old wooden box back home, and I somehow never thought of trying the tall, shiny new phone that sat on the table in the hall.

As I grew into my teens, the memories of those childhood conversations never really left me. Often, in moments of doubt and perplexity, I would recall the serene sense of security I had then. I appreciated now how patient, understanding, and kind she was to have spent her time on a little boy.

A few years later, on my way west to college, my plane put down in Seattle. I had about half an hour between planes. I spent fifteen minutes or so on the phone with my sister, who lived there now. Then, without thinking what I was doing, I dialed my hometown operator.

"Information Please," I said.

Miraculously, I heard the small voice I remembered so well.

I hadn't planned this, but I heard myself saying, "Could you please tell me how to spell 'fix'?"

There was a long pause. Then came the soft-spoken answer, "I guess your finger must have healed by now."

I laughed. "So it's really still you," I said. "I wonder if you have any idea how much you meant to me during that time?"

"I wonder," she said, "if you know how much your calls meant to me? I never had any children, and I used to look forward to your calls."

I told her how often I had thought of her over the years, and I asked if I could call her again when I came back to visit my sister.

"Please do," she said. "Just ask for Sally."

Three months later I was back in Seattle. A different voice answered, "Information."

I asked for Sally.

"Are you a friend?" she asked.

"Yes, a very old friend," I answered.

"I'm sorry to have to tell you this," she said. "Sally had been working part-time the last few years because she was sick. She died five weeks ago."

Before I could hang up, she said, "Wait a minute. Did you say your name was Paul?"

"Yes."

"Well, Sally left a message for you. She wrote it down in

case you called. Let me read it to you. The note says, 'Tell him I still say there are other worlds to sing in. He'll know what I mean.'"

———

Submitted by Toni Chambers

Friendship

*O*ur friendship cannot rely on our past together. And it cannot rely on the future we anticipate. It must be now. It must be today. For our past is only precious memories, and our future is still misty imaginings. Can't we find time to be together today?

———

Mary Hollingsworth
Just Between Friends

A Father's Plea

On Thursday, May 27, 1999, Darrell Scott, the father of Rachel Scott, a victim of the Columbine High School shootings in Littleton, Colorado, was invited to address the House Judiciary Committee's subcommittee. What he said to our national leaders during this special session of Congress was painful but truthful. The following is a portion of the transcript:

"Since the dawn of creation there has been both good and evil in the hearts of men and women. We all contain the seeds of kindness and the seeds of violence. The death of my wonderful daughter, Rachel Joy Scott, and the deaths of that heroic teacher, and the other eleven children who died must not be in vain. Their blood cries out for answers. The first recorded act of violence was when Cain slew his brother Abel out in the field. The villain was not the club he used. Neither was it the fault of the NCA, the National Club Association. The true killer was Cain, and the reason for the murder could only be found in Cain's heart.

"In the days that followed the Columbine tragedy, I was

amazed at how quickly fingers began to be pointed at groups such as the National Rifle Association (NRA). I am not a member of the NRA. I am not a hunter. I do not even own a gun. I am not here to represent or defend the NRA. I don't believe that they are responsible for my daughter's death. Therefore I do not believe that they need to be defended. If I believed they had anything to do with Rachel's murder, I would be their strongest opponent. I am here today to declare that Columbine was not just a tragedy—it was a spiritual event that should be forcing us to look at where the real blame lies. Much of the blame lies here in this room. Much of the blame lies behind the pointing fingers of the accusers themselves.

"I wrote a poem just four nights ago that expresses my feelings best. This was written long before I knew I would be speaking here today.

> Your laws ignore our deepest needs.
> Your words are empty air.
> You've stripped away our heritage;
> You've outlawed simple prayer.
> Now gunshots fill our classrooms,
> And precious children die.
> You seek for answers everywhere
> And ask the question, "Why?"
> You regulate restrictive laws
> Through legislative creed,

And yet you fail to understand
That God is what we need!

"Men and women are three-part beings. We all consist of body, soul, and spirit. When we refuse to acknowledge a third of our makeup, we create a void that allows evil, prejudice, and hatred to rush in and wreak havoc. Spiritual influences were present within our educational systems for most of our nation's history. Many of our major colleges began as theological seminaries. This is historical fact.

"What has happened to us as a nation? We have refused to honor God, and in doing so, we open the doors to hatred and violence. And when something as terrible as Columbine's tragedy occurs, politicians immediately look for a scapegoat, such as the NRA. They immediately seek to pass more restrictive laws that contribute to erode away our personal and private liberties.

"We don't need more restrictive laws. Eric and Dylan would not have been stopped by metal detectors. No amount of gun laws can stop someone who spends months planning this type of massacre. The real villain lies within our own hearts. Political posturing and restrictive legislation are not the answers. The young people of our nation hold the key. There is a spiritual awakening taking place that will not be squelched.

"We do not need more religion. We do not need more gaudy television evangelists spewing out religious garbage.

We do not need more million-dollar church buildings built while people with basic needs are being ignored. We *do* need a change of heart and an humble acknowledgment that this nation was founded on the principle of simple trust in God.

"As my son Craig lay under that table in the school library and saw his two friends murdered before his very eyes, he did not hesitate to pray in school. I defy any law or politician to deny him that right! I challenge every young person in America and around the world to realize that on April 20, 1999, at Columbine High School, prayer was brought back to our schools.

"Do not let the many prayers offered by those students be in vain. Dare to move into the new millennium with a sacred disregard for legislation that violates your God-given right to communicate with him. To those of you who would point your finger at the NRA, I give to you a sincere challenge. Dare to examine your own heart before casting the first stone. My daughter's death will not be in vain. The young people of this country will not allow that to happen."

———

Darrell Scott

Overheard

Overheard outside the junior section of a public library, two little girls were talking.

One remarked, "Yes, we've moved into a new house now, so my brother and I have a room each."

Then she added thoughtfully: "But Mommy still has to sleep with Daddy."

———

Nigel Rees

Because of You

*O*n a black, stormy Alabama night, just before midnight, an older African-American woman was standing on the side of the highway. The rain was lashing against her, and she was looking around desperately for help.

Her car had broken down, and she was terribly frightened and alone, badly in need of a ride. Soaking wet, she decided to try and flag down the next car that came along.

A young Caucasian man stopped to help her, which was generally unheard of in those conflict-filled 1960s. The man took her to safety, helped her get assistance, and put her into a taxi. She seemed to be in a big hurry. Still, she took the time to write down his address and thanked him profusely.

Seven days went by and a knock came at the man's front door. To his surprise, a giant, console, color television set was being delivered to his home. His name was graciously written on a special note that was attached to the TV. Here's what it said:

Thank you so much for assisting me on the highway the other night. The rain drenched not only my clothes, but also my spirits. Then you came along. Because of you, I was able to make it to my dying husband's bedside just before he passed away. God bless you for helping me and unselfishly serving others.

Mrs. Nat King Cole
TRUE KINDNESS IS COLOR BLIND.

———

Written with facts from public records

The Discovery

*O*nce there was a young monk, who graduated from his early training and was sent to the monastery for scribes. There he lived with the other monks as an assistant scribe for several years.

At long last the monk, now middle-aged, became qualified to work as a scribe himself. And the old monk in charge of the manuscript copying took him to his new desk. There he found all the tools he needed to make copies of the sacred Scriptures, including a copy of the original text.

Looking at the copy, the new scribe frowned.

"What's wrong, my son?" asked the old monk.

"Why do we work from a *copy* of the original Scriptures? Wouldn't it be safer and more accurate to work from the original itself? What if someone accidentally made a mistake in the copy?"

The old monk looked at him with a surprised look. No one had ever intimated before that a mistake could have been made in copying. Still, the question had merit, so he said he would investigate it himself.

The old monk left the copying room and went to the cata-combs below the monastery in search of the original manu-script of the Scriptures. He was gone for many hours. Finally, the younger monks became concerned for his safety and went in search of him.

When they found the old monk, deep in a small room of the labyrinth of tunnels beneath the monastery, he was slumped over the precious old manuscripts weeping loudly.

Rushing to him, the younger monk asked, "What's wrong, brother? Are you all right?"

Glancing up through tear-streaked eyes, the old monk pointed at a particular section of the manuscript and sobbed, "You were right. Look. The word is 'celebrate'!"

Originator Unknown

Seven-Year-Old Beauty

✀

A seven-year-old girl was watching her mother put on some face cream and asked, "Mommy, is that the cream they show on the television that makes you beautiful?"

When her mommy told her it was, the little girl commented, after a thoughtful pause, "When is it supposed to start working?"

———

Arthur Marshall

A Conversation between Moses and God

*E*xcuse me, sir."

"Is that you again, Moses?"

"I'm afraid it is, sir."

"What is it this time, Moses? More computer problems?"

"How did you guess?"

"I don't have to guess, Moses. Remember?"

"Oh yeah, I forgot."

"Tell me what you want, Moses."

"But you already know. Remember?"

"Moses!"

"Sorry, sir."

"Well, go ahead, Moses. Spit it out!"

"Well, I have a question, sir. You know those ten *things* you sent me?"

"You mean the commandments, Moses?"

"That's it. I was wondering if they were important."

"What do you mean 'were important,' Moses? Of course,

they are important. Otherwise I wouldn't have sent them to you."

"Well, sorry, but I lost them. I could say the dog ate them, but of course you would see right through that, sir."

"What do you mean 'you lost them'? Are you trying to tell me you didn't save them, Moses?"

"No sir. I forgot."

"Well, my Son always saves, Moses."

"Yeah, I know. You told me before. I was going to, but I forgot. I did send them to some people before I lost them though."

"And did you hear back from any of them?"

"You already know I did. What about the one who said he never uses 'shalt not,' can he change the words a little bit?"

"Yes, Moses. As long as he doesn't change the meaning."

"And what about the guy who thought your stance was a little harsh and recommended calling them the Ten Suggestions or letting people pick one or two to try for a while?"

"Moses, I'll pretend I didn't hear that."

"I think that means no. Well, what about the guy who said I was scamming him?"

"I think that is *spamming*, Moses."

"Oh yeah. I e-mailed him back and told him I don't even eat that stuff and I have no idea how you can send it to someone through a computer."

"And what did he say?"

"You know what he said. He used your name in vain. You don't think he might have sent me one of those plagues and that's the reason I lost those ten things, do you?"

"They're called viruses, Moses."

"Whatever. This computer stuff is just too much for me. Can we just go back to those stone tablets? It was hard on my back taking them out and reading them each day, but I never lost them."

"We'll do it the new way, Moses."

"I was afraid you'd say that, sir."

"Moses, what did I tell you to do if you messed up?"

"You told me to hold up this rat and stretch it out toward the computer."

"It's a mouse, Moses. Mouse! Mouse! And did you do that?"

"No, I decided to try the technical support first. After all, who knows more about this stuff than you, and I really like your hours. By the way, sir, did Noah have two of these mice on the ark?"

"No, Moses."

"One other thing. Why didn't you name them frogs instead of mice, because didn't you tell me they sit on a pad?"

"I didn't name them, Moses. Man did, and you can call yours a frog if you want to."

"Oh, that explains it. Kind of like Adam, huh, sir? I bet some woman told him to call it a mouse. After all, wasn't it a woman who named one of the computers Apple?"

"Say good-night, Moses."

"Wait a minute, sir. I am stretching out the mouse, and it seems to be working. Yes, a couple of the ten things have come back."

"Which ones are they, Moses?"

"Let's see. 'Thou shalt not steal from any grave an image' and 'Thou shalt not uncover thy neighbor's wife.'"

"Turn the computer off, Moses. I'm sending you another set of stone tablets. How does 'Same Day Air' sound?"

The Ant and the Contact Lens

$\mathcal{A}$ young woman named Brenda was invited to go rock climbing. Although she was scared to death, she went with her group to a tremendous granite cliff. In spite of her fear, Brenda put on the climbing gear, took hold of the rope, and started up the face of that rock.

She finally reached a ledge where she could take a breather. As she was hanging there, the safety rope snapped against Brenda's eye and knocked out her contact lens. So, there she was on a rock ledge, with hundreds of feet below her and hundreds of feet above her . . . and no contact lens.

Of course, she looked and looked, hoping the lens had landed on the ledge, but it just wasn't there. Far from home, terrified of the height, and now with her sight blurry, she was desperate and began to get upset. So she prayed to the Lord to help her find the lens.

When Brenda got to the top of the cliff, a friend examined her eye and her clothing for the lens, but there was no contact lens to be found. She sat down, despondent, waiting for the rest of the party to make it up the face of the cliff.

She looked out across range after range of mountains, thinking of that Bible verse that says, "The eyes of the Lord run to and fro throughout the whole earth."

She thought, *Lord, you can see all these mountains. You know every stone and leaf, and you know exactly where my contact lens is. Please help me.*

Finally, they walked down the trail to the bottom. At the bottom there was a new party of climbers just starting up the face of the cliff.

One of them shouted out, "Hey, you guys! Anybody lose a contact lens?"

That would have been startling enough, but do you know why the climber saw it? An ant was moving slowly across the face of the rock, carrying it.

Brenda said that her father is a cartoonist. When she told him the incredible story of the ant, the prayer, and the contact lens, he drew a picture of an ant lugging that contact lens with the words, "Lord, I don't know why you want me to carry this thing. I can't eat it, and it's awfully heavy. But if this is what you want me to do, I'll carry it for you."

It would probably do some of us good to occasionally say, "God, I don't know why you want me to carry this load. I can see no good in it, and it's awfully heavy. But, if you want me to carry it, I will."

God doesn't call the qualified; he qualifies the called.

———

A true story by Josh and Karen Zarandona

What's behind Door Number 2?

$\mathcal{M}$any years ago I was involved with a great evangelistic program called Campaigns for Christ. Several times I joined large groups of Christians who traveled to specific destinations and conducted month-long outreach efforts. In those days, the method we used was to go door to door and talk with people, setting up Bible studies that we conducted in their homes.

Now, if you've never had the pleasure of knocking on doors and meeting strangers for Christ, you've missed one of the more terrifying and rewarding aspects of Christianity. While most people are friendly and polite, there are always a few surprises along the way. It reminded me of the old TV show *Let's Make a Deal,* because you never knew what would be behind the next door. It might be a great prize—a sincere soul who was searching for Christ—or *not.* The suspense kept us on our toes. Personally, I'd rather do a Texas line dance on a bed of hot coals with no boots on than knock on doors, but I was willing to do it for Jesus.

One of the most memorable campaigns for me was to

Wellington, New Zealand, where I later moved and lived for a time as a missionary. I loved the country and the wonderful Christians I met there, some of whom I still contact on a fairly regular basis. And the campaign there was very successful, with over a hundred people coming to Christ.

I remember one late afternoon, just before time to stop knocking on doors for the day and go to dinner. We were tired, my feet hurt, and we were hungry. My door-knocking partner, Rob, and I walked up on the porch of a pretty, white clapboard house—the last house at the end of the block—and did what we were trained to do: We knocked on the door. It was my turn to talk to the person who might answer the door; so I took a half-step forward, and my partner stepped back slightly. Then we waited, tract and Bible in hand. As usual I was thinking, *Wouldn't it be great if nobody was home.* (The Cowardly Lion has nothing on me!)

Suddenly my scaredy-cat thoughts were interrupted by the wooden door being jerked open. Before I could say hello, and in one fluid motion, an older woman, whose countenance was less than inviting, latched the screen door and growled, "I know who you are, because my neighbor called me, and I'm not interested! Me got me own religion!" Then she slammed the door in our faces, and we heard the deadbolt lock snap into place with finality.

Without reacting or moving, to the closed wooden door I said calmly, "Thank you so much for your time and hospitality. We have enjoyed our visit with you. Have a nice day, and may the Lord bless you." When I turned around, my partner was cracking up with laughter.

We stepped off the porch, had a good laugh, and walked around the end of the block to the house that backed up to the one we had just left. This would be our last house for the day. Happily, this time it was Rob's turn to talk to the person; so I stepped back, and he stepped up. I noticed that the wooden door was standing open, and there was a half-glass-and-half-screen door closed. We could vaguely see into the dimly lit living room. Rob knocked on the door, and we waited.

Suddenly, from somewhere inside the house, we heard a loud, deep "Woof!" Then we heard the pounding of a four-footed animal that sounded as if it should be wearing a saddle. Kathump! Kathump! "Woof! Woof!" And out of the darkness arose a huge Great Dane that reared up and put his monstrous paws and angry, barking face on the glass-and-screen door. He was so big that his paws were directly in Rob's face, and he punctuated his pounce against the flimsy door with another gigantic "Woof!" I took two steps toward the porch steps, looking for somewhere to run.

Without blinking or moving, Rob calmly said, "Good afternoon, sir; we just met your sister around the corner."

I lost it! I fell off the porch, literally, laughing my head off. Then Rob lost his composure and lapsed into hysteria with me. As he picked up my Bible and helped me up, and amidst our gales of laughter, the woman who lived there came to the door. We had quite a time trying to explain what we were doing in a hysterical fit in her front yard, much less talk to her seriously about the Lord.

You never know what the Lord will have waiting for you behind Door Number 2!

Another Day, Another Door

*T*here were lots of other crazy things that happened to us while knocking doors for Christ through the years. One little, old farmer from Kansas, who had never been off his wheat farm, had some of the most eye-opening experiences. His name was Harold, and he was in his early seventies.

One day shy, reserved Harold was knocking doors with Rob—a crazy, never-met-a-stranger Kiwi (a native New Zealander). As Rob tells it, he and Harold walked up the steps onto the porch of a large brick-and-wood house in a wealthy neighborhood, and Rob rang the doorbell. Then they waited. They could hear someone shuffling around in the house, but it was a long time before the wooden door opened.

The attractive, young woman of the house pushed the door wide open and smiled at them brightly. She was topless. Not to be befuddled by the brashness of the woman, Rob— keeping his eyes locked on her face—calmly talked to her about the Lord. As he said later, she obviously needed to know Christ badly. Meanwhile, Rob said Harold's jaw dropped all the way to his knees, where it stayed until the conversation was over and he stumbled off the porch.

It was a long day for Harold.

The next day, Harold and I were working together. We climbed some rickety wooden stairs at the side of a house and stood on a small porch. It was Harold's turn to talk, so I stepped back, and he knocked on the door.

When the two occupants came to the door, it was a gay couple, one of whom was in a dress and had long hair. Harold, to his credit I thought, held a very calm, competent conversation with the two men. As I suspected early in the conversation, they were not interested in the Lord or his Word; so we left our tract, wished them well, and walked down the stairs to the sidewalk.

As we headed for the next house, I discovered why Harold had been so kind and patient with the gay couple. He said, "That sure was a homely woman, wasn't it?"

He gave me a really puzzled look when I laughingly responded, "Toto, we're not in Kansas anymore!"

It was a long campaign for Harold.

Where's Frankie?

Little Frankie was a classic toddler. One day he pulled a chair over to the front window and carefully placed it inside the drapes. He was standing there staring out at the world when his mother came looking for him.

She finally spied his little white legs protruding beneath the drapes and quietly slipped in behind him. Then she heard him speaking to himself in very somber terms.

He was saying, "I've *got* to get out of here!"

———

James Dobson
Parenting Isn't for Cowards

81

Fraidy Cat

We got her at the place for friendless or abandoned animals—a tiny gray-and-white kitten whose eyes were still blue. Just an alley cat, nameless, homeless, too young to lap milk from a saucer—we had to feed her with an eyedropper. She didn't like the strange new world in which she found herself. She hid under the bed and cried. We laughed and called her Fraidy Cat.

She soon got used to us, of course. She slept a lot and played games with balls of wadded paper. I never saw her chase her tail, as kittens are supposed to do. But she had a good time.

She had an even better time when we moved to the country. She was half-grown then and liked to stalk things in the tall grass behind the house. Twice she brought home a mouse for us to admire, and once, a bird. Fortunately the bird wasn't hurt, so we took it away from her and let it go. She seemed to think our distinction between mice and birds was pretty silly. Logically, she was right.

She was an aloof little beast in those days—I say "little"

because she remained a very small cat. She didn't show much affection for anyone. In fact, if you tried to pet her when she wasn't in the mood, she would dig her claws in harder than was pleasant, or even bite. This didn't bother me, of course, because I am really a dog man. I can take cats or leave them alone.

We acquired a dog soon after we moved to the country, a friendly boxer named Major. Fraidy loathed him. For the first month or so, if he came too close, she would spit and rake his nose, leaving him hurt and bewildered. I was rather indignant about this—after all, I'm a dog man—and I slapped Fraidy once or twice for assaulting Major. "Who do you think you are?" I asked her. "Try to remember you're nothing but a cat!"

While she was still too young, in our opinion, for such goings-on, Fraidy decided to become a mother. When the time came, however, she didn't hide away like most cats; she stuck close to us. Maybe she had a hunch it was going to be tough. It was. There was only a single kitten, much too big. She couldn't handle it herself; I had to help her. It took all my strength, and I thought she would bite me, but she didn't. She just watched me, her yellow eyes glassy with pain. Afterwards, she licked my hand. But the kitten was born dead.

"Never mind, Fraidy," we said. "You'll have better luck next time."

For days she was gaunt and thin; she looked for the kitten everywhere. I believe she thought Major was responsible for its disappearance—all her old distrust of him came back, for a while. She got over that, but one thing she did not get over: her gratitude to me. She followed me from room to room, and if I sat down she would jump into my lap, put her forefeet on my chest, and stare into my face with the most soulful look imaginable.

"Typical woman," my wife said, laughing. "In love with her obstetrician."

"It's just misplaced maternal instinct," I said. "She'll get over it as soon as she has some kittens."

Nature, it seemed, had the same idea, because before very long Fraidy was pregnant again. We figured she would have at least two kittens, this time. Smaller ones. We were very happy for her. She seemed sleepy and satisfied.

Then one day, not long ago, she developed a cough. We thought nothing of it; her appetite was good. She seemed somewhat lethargic, but after all, her time was almost due. Then, early yesterday morning, she came up from the kitchen where she slept and jumped on our bed. She curled up in my lap and looked at me. She meowed unhappily.

"What's the matter with this fool cat?" I said. "What's she trying to tell us?"

All yesterday she didn't eat. She even refused water. In the evening, finally, I called a vet. There are good vets, I guess, and bad ones. This one—when he saw her—said it seemed to be just a cold. No fever. Nothing very wrong. That was yesterday.

This morning Fraidy Cat dragged herself upstairs again, but this time she couldn't jump onto the bed. She was too weak. The roof of her mouth was very pale; her eyes were glazed.

I telephoned another vet. It was Sunday morning, and early, but he said to bring her over. I did. He examined her carefully. He knew his business; you can always tell.

"I'm sorry," he said. "Uterine infection. I'm afraid the kittens are dead."

"Can't you operate?" I said. "Can't you save her?"

He shook his head. "I could try. But it would just prolong things. She's pretty far gone now." He looked at my face. He was a kind man, and he loved animals. "I'd put her away," he said gently, "if I were you."

After a while I nodded my head.

"Now?" said the vet, "or after you've gone?"

"I'll stay with her," I said.

He brought the hypodermic needle and the Nembutal. "It doesn't hurt," he said. "She'll go to sleep, that's all." The needle went home, quick and merciful.

She was just an ordinary alley cat. She had no pedigree, no clever tricks. But I remembered how she'd roll over on the path when we'd drive up in the car. I remembered how she loved to eat slivers of melon from our breakfast plates. I remembered how she liked to have her ears scratched, and how she licked my hand the day I had to hurt her so terribly, the day her kitten was born dead.

I stood there with my hand touching her so that perhaps she would not be afraid. "It's all right, Fraidy," I said. "Go to sleep. Go to sleep." And at last she put her head down on her clean little paws and closed her eyes.

I felt blindly for my pocketbook. It wasn't there. "I haven't any money," I said. "I'll have to send it to you."

"That's all right," the vet said. "Don't bother."

I touched her ear for the last time and turned back to the door. It was a golden summer morning, calm, serene. Down in the meadow a gigantic willow tree made a burst of greenness against the sky.

I got in the car quickly and drove away. But not far down the road I stopped the car and put my forehead against the steering wheel and wept. Because she was such a little cat. Because she had tried to tell me that she was sick, that she was in trouble, and I hadn't helped her. Not until too late. And I felt the awful emptiness that comes from not knowing how much you love something until you have lost it.

———

Arthur Gordon
A Touch of Wonder

*F*athers are those who give
daughters away to other men
who aren't nearly good enough,
so they can have grandchildren
who are smarter than anybody's.

———

Paul Harvey

Oh! If only we could learn
to "love past" things as children do—
wrinkles, warts, handicaps, skin colors,
blunderings, cultural differences,
a grandparent's funny underwear,
and even meanness.
Then the world would be
a fit place to live.

———

Mary Hollingsworth
On Raising Children

Wunny Wace

When my cousin Donna first learned to talk, she had a bit of difficulty making the *f* sound. She automatically substituted the *w* sound for an *f*. So, instead of "foot," she said her "woot" hurt. And in popular fairy tales, things were "war, war away."

Donna loved my brother, Frank, who was a teenager at the time. She called him "Wank." And he teased her unmercifully, which she objected to loudly with fake indignance.

Frank would say, "Donna, you're a funny face."

And she would say, "I'm *not* a wunny wace."

He would say, "You're a big, fat elephant."

And she would reply, with feeling, "I'm *not* a big, wat elewant!"

He would say, "Your face is full of freckles."

And she said, "My wace is *not* wull o' wreckles!"

This game went on for years every time our two families were together until Donna's sixth birthday. We came to celebrate with her. She opened her gifts. We played games with the children at the party. And we had cake and ice cream.

After the party was over, Frank, in standard form, said, "Donna, you're still a funny face."

And to his surprise . . . and ours, she said, "I am not a funny face"—the *f* sound clear and accurate.

"Well, what happened to my 'wunny wace'?" he laughed.

And to everyone's amazement she said, "I'm six years old now. I don't have to talk like that anymore." And from that day on, she never did again.

Wamilies! Aren't they wabulous?

You Don't Know Me, But . . .

✧

*E*dmund Gosse, author of *Father and Son,* was traveling on a bus one day in the 1880s, and a lady, who was headmistress of the local school, got on the bus. She sat down next to a very respectable town attorney and electrified the whole busload of passengers by saying to him, "I can see you don't know who I am, but you are the father of one of my children."

———

Ann Thwaite

The Torn Bible

When I was a tiny girl, I was taught by my mom and minister dad to take care of my little Bible. They taught me to love the Word of God and treat it with careful respect. I wasn't supposed to get it dirty. I was not allowed to tear or bend its little pages. And I was never, ever to draw pictures in it with my crayons.

One summer a preacher friend of my dad's, F. I. Stanley, was speaking in a nearby tent meeting in a little community called Old Tarrant, Texas. So, as we often did, especially in the summer, our family drove the few miles to Old Tarrant to hear him preach. His topic that evening was respect for God's Word.

My family sat on the front row, right in front of the big, wooden podium, since my dad was leading the singing that night. I can remember that we were so close, Brother Stanley was so tall, and I was so small, that I had to look almost straight up to see Brother Stanley's face.

To illustrate his point of how some people fail to respect God's Word by ignoring what it says, he used an inexpensive, small, child-size Bible. He would read a verse of Scripture that people often ignore, and to emphasize his point, he would tear that page out of the little Bible and toss it on the floor. I can vividly remember those little pages falling to the floor right at my feet.

I was extremely upset by that sermon, especially his tearing up the Bible. And I complained loudly about it to my mother, who tried to keep me quiet during the service. A few days later, F. I. Stanley came to our house for lunch. My mom related to him the traumatic effect his sermon illustration had had on me. He admitted that it had never crossed his mind that children would misunderstand his point, and he promised to never use that illustration again.

Ironically, he was making the exact same point that my parents had been making with me, just using opposite logic, and over the years, both have come to mean a lot to me.

"The word of the Lord is flawless."
(2 Samuel 22:31)

God's Funeral

The great reformer, Martin Luther, was once going through a period of depression and discouragement. For days his long face graced the family table and dampened the family's home life.

One day his wife came to the breakfast table all dressed in black, as if she were going to a funeral service. When Martin asked her who had died, she replied, "Martin, the way you've been behaving lately, I thought God had died; so I came prepared to attend his funeral."

Her gentle but effective rebuke drove straight to Luther's heart, and as a result of that lesson, he resolved never again to allow worldly care, resentment, depression, discouragement, or frustration to defeat him. By God's grace, he vowed, he would submit his life to the Savior and reflect his grace in a spirit of rejoicing, whatever came.

Luther determined to shout with Paul, "Thanks be to God! He gives us the victory through our Lord Jesus Christ" (1 Corinthians 15:57).

Billy Graham, Unto the Hills

Sands of Time

✦

$\mathcal{I}$ once knew of some people called Sands. They lived overlooking the seaside, and Mr. Sands decreed in his will that when he died he was to be cremated and his ashes scattered over the, er, sands. And so it turned out, though not quite in the way he expected.

Shortly after his cremation, a small group of his relatives was seen trooping down to the shore carrying the casket containing his ashes. After they had stood in silent prayer for a minute or so, the lid was removed. At that very moment, a gust of wind whipped the ashes out of the casket and blew them over the family.

But Mr. Sands had had his wish—even if his ashes were scattered over the Sands rather than over the, er, sands.

———

As told to Nigel Rees

95

Go home to your family
and tell them how much
the Lord has done for you,
and how he has had mercy on you.

———

Mark 5:19

Terror of Buccaneer Bay

*T*hat's what he was—the Terror of Buccaneer Bay. Strong men paled when he approached. Yet, to look at him, you'd never guess that he was more dreaded in the little Anchorage inlet than a hurricane.

He was about half my age, eighteen or so. Tousled blond hair, tall and slender, a nose that went askew when he laughed, and—until that incredible Black Friday—a friendly half-smile on his lips. His eyes should have warned me. They were the blue eyes of a dreamer with a seagoing urge. A dreamer who never had enough sea room. Sometimes I wondered if the whole Atlantic would have been enough.

I saw him first at the club dock when I was adjusting the jib stay of my *Lightning* for the coming race. I heard a cheery "Hello!" and looked up, and there he was.

"Hi," I said, wondering if he were a newcomer to the Buccaneer Bay colony, or just a visitor.

"A fine looking sailboat you've got there," he said. "Are you a member of the Yacht Club?"

"Well, sort of," I admitted.

"Sort of? What do you mean by that?"

I looked up impatiently. But you couldn't get mad at that friendly smile. "I work around here each summer," I told him. "Helps get me through college. The fellows threw in a special membership without charge."

"My folks have rented the Murray cottage. I want to join the Yacht Club. I want to get the biggest sailboat I can get for my money," he said.

"Better learn to sail first," I said.

"But how do you know I can't sail?"

I laughed. "A sailor never calls a sailboat a sailboat. And a smart sailor never tries to buy the biggest boat for his money. He tries to get the smallest."

He looked at me as though I were crazy. I explained: "Too much boat for your money means a rotten hull, poor rigging, and a bag of headaches. How much do you want to spend?"

"All I've got saved, about two thousand dollars."

I advised him where to buy a good secondhand boat and again cautioned him to get a small, quality boat.

A week later I was doing a varnish job on a swank cruiser that belonged to H. Maynard Steele. By this time I knew my new friend's name was Archy Duval, and I guess he'd discovered my name, for he came down to the dock and said excitedly, "Hi, Bob. I've bought a boat."

He had that dreamy look again as he pointed out his purchase—the *Crazy Lady*.

My heart sank. She was a beaut to look at, a forty-foot sloop, but those of us who hung out around the basin knew she was riddled with dry rot inside, that worms feasted on her planking, and that her auxiliary engine was an asthmatic old coffee grinder. And her rigging was rotten.

Archy took my bad news about the *Crazy Lady* pretty gamely. He gulped and said, "Maybe you're right, but she's mine, and I'm going to sail her until she goes under. Will you help me learn to sail her?"

I helped him. I didn't want to, but I couldn't resist that appeal in his blue eyes. So I spent the afternoon explaining the basics of lowering and raising sails and how to use the little engine to get around in the narrow breakwater entrance to our basin. When we tied up near his cottage, I begged only one thing of him.

"For Pete's sake, get a ten-foot dinghy and learn to sail before you take the *Crazy Lady* out."

"But you just taught me how to sail," he objected.

I shuddered. If Archy thought he could sail after one short afternoon on a flat sea with a small breeze, there was trouble ahead.

Came Friday, still called "Black Friday" at Buccaneer Bay, I was helping H. Maynard Steele as a deck hand on his cruiser, the *Black Douglas*. I noticed the *Crazy Lady* was not at her moorings. Even as I went to get the binoculars to look for her, I knew that Archy had gone against my advice and was out "sailing."

She was about a mile outside the breakwater, and her mainsail was jibbing violently, and I winced at knowing what a beating the rotten rigging must be taking. Then I focused on Archy at the tiller. No sailor should ever take out a forty-foot sloop without a deckhand.

I prayed that Mr. Steele and his friends would hurry and board so we could get out of the narrow breakwater before Archy approached.

"Better keep an eye on that sloop heading in, sir," I said. "There's just one man aboard, and he doesn't know a sheet from a halyard."

Mr. Steele whistled. "You don't suppose he'll enter the basin under sail?"

"Oh no!" I shouted. The *Crazy Lady* was headed for the rocks in full sail with Archy trying frantically to get the sail down. Finally he saw his course and ran back and gave the tiller a yank just in time. But now the *Crazy Lady* bore directly down on us.

Mr. Steele threw both his engines in reverse and tried to get out of the path of the oncoming boat. There was room for the *Crazy Lady* to clear us in the narrow channel if he didn't mess with the sail, but that's just what he did. It was almost as if the sloop careened around and tore in for the kill.

Mr. Steele jammed his engines in forward and turned us just in time to avoid a head-on collision, but as the *Crazy Lady* shot by us, the end of her boom carved a splintering white gash in the polished side of the cruiser.

Above the thunderous roar of Mr. Steele's anger, I heard Archy yell, "What do I do?"

"Bring her into the wind and cut your halyard," I shouted.

"Tell him to cut his throat!" bellowed Mr. Steele.

Archy ducked below, presumably to get a knife. The *Crazy Lady* leaped joyously ahead, aiming unerringly for a boat that was heading unsuspectingly toward the bay. Hoarse shouts of alarm from the crew brought Archy back up and not a second too soon. He seized the tiller and avoided more than a glancing blow. Archy was shouting his apologies across the sizzling atmosphere when the *Crazy Lady* was bearing down on an express cruiser riding at anchor. Boats scattered, horns were honking to warn the unwary. But the boats unattended at their moorings could do nothing but wait stoically for whatever blows fate might bring.

The *Crazy Lady* made havoc as she charged gaily from one direction to another, shearing boats in her path, careening against a couple of helpless yawls, and clipping the top gear off a fishing vessel.

The *Black Douglas*, with Mr. Steele grimly determined at the wheel, was closing in on the *Crazy Lady*. "I'll sink Archy Duval," he muttered. "Get that anchor ready and when we go by and he yells for a life preserver, throw him that anchor."

He looked at me. "If you miss him, you're fired."

Fate intervened. Archy found a knife and was slashing at the main halyard as we neared. A speedboat rushed in to help, and Archy was towed to his moorings by grim-lipped men who said little but said that little very well indeed.

I went around to see Archy that night to give him the bad news that the Yacht Club was rejecting his application. They were also offering Archy's parents double their money for their cottage if they would just leave town.

I heard a note of pride in his voice. "Dad said we weren't running away. And he told me to stick to the *Crazy Lady* until I became the best sailor in Buccaneer Bay."

Archy was up against a lot. People were calling him the Terror of Buccaneer Bay; they shunned him in town although no one was deliberately cruel. But Archy stuck to his dream. Every day, in all kinds of weather, he'd chug out of the break-water and practice. He even had the old rigging replaced.

"I love that old tub," he admitted to me one day. "I love every rotten plank in her. I know she won't last another sea-son, but I'll stick with her until she sinks."

Prophetic words! Fortunately for my peace of mind, I didn't know that I'd be with him when the time came.

The hurricane struck a week later. We knew it was com-ing, of course, we just didn't know which direction it would come from. If it came from the north we'd get the wind from the land and we'd be protected in our basin. But if it came from the south, we'd get the full force from the ocean and the little breakwater would be buried under a tidal wave of raging sea, and every boat in the basin would be wrecked.

An hour before dark, we heard the news: The hurricane

would strike from the south, and we needed to get all the boats across the bay. Everybody had been ready for hours, and we all started for the boats. The telephone stopped me. It was Mr. Steele. He wanted me to help him take the *Black Douglas* across the bay.

"Sorry," I told him. "I'm going to help with the *Crazy Lady*."

The telephone receiver grew hot in my hands. I hung up. I knew Mr. Steele could get other help. Archy couldn't.

He was just bringing his old engine coughing and sputtering to life when he saw me. His look of astonishment turned to gratitude when he realized I was there to help him.

"I don't believe I could make it by myself," he said humbly, a far cry from his first know-it-all attitude.

As we headed for the narrow entrance to the breakwater I took off the sailcovers. If that old engine broke down we'd need the sails in a hurry to have enough power to clear the breakwater and avoid the rocks.

I looked back. The *Crazy Lady* would be the first to reach the narrows, and the *Black Douglas* was right behind us with dozens of other boats jockeying for position.

Then it happened. The old engine went dead and Archy and I sprang to the mainsail and worked feverishly. Wind and sea were carrying us back into the narrow breakwater entrance. Even as I leaped to action I knew there was no chance of raising the sail in time to steer away before we hit the south side of the entrance. The mainsail was halfway up when our stern grounded on a rock with a sickening thud.

Now the sail was worse than useless as it held us on the rocks as each succeeding swell threw us higher and higher on the rocks.

"Here comes the *Black Douglas,*" shouted Archy. "She can throw us a line and haul us off."

As the trim cruiser eased its way through the breakwater I shouted for help. Mr. Steele just looked at us.

"Are you sure you can't get off?" he yelled.

"If you don't get us off right now, we're done for," I answered him.

"Best news I've heard in years," he shouted back, and with a burst of speed the *Black Douglas* shot through the break-water and out into the bay.

Archy and I stared at each other in unbelieving consterna-tion. Fortunately Jack Stuart's powerful fishing vessel approached the entrance, and I knew Jack wouldn't let us down.

Moments later with a two-inch towing line attached, Jack pulled the line taut and gave his boat the soup.

The strong vessel pulled our bow away from the rocks, and then the stern came free and we were sitting obliquely across the entrance. Archy gave a heart-rending yell and pointed down into the cabin.

I looked. I gasped. A hole big enough for a whale had been punched in our starboard bow. The whole Atlantic was rush-ing in. I turned to scream at Jack to get his boat through the breakwater before we sank and blocked the entrance.

But it was too late. The *Crazy Lady* gave a sigh of frustration and sank. But the spirit of Black Friday was still with her, for her last act before she sank was to turn broadside to the narrow breakwater entrance. She closed it as surely as a cork closes a bottle.

Archy and I scrambled up the mast. We could see that Jack's boat was trapped inside the breakwater, with no chance of escaping across the bay to the leeside. And the hurricane would be here in minutes.

Jack threw us a line and we were pulled aboard like a couple of drowned rats. Jack didn't say much as he watched the two dozen or so boats that had been heading for the safety of the bay turn around in disgust. He said more in awe than anger, "Never before has so much been done to so many by so few."

"Go below and you'll find some dry clothes," Jack said, not unkindly. "On second thought, stay below till we get back to the dock. I'll tell them you're drowned. It'll make them feel better."

I tried to cheer Archy up. What the *Crazy Lady* had done that Black Friday was nothing compared to what she'd done today. We let him off at his dock and then went on to the Yacht Club to prepare for the worst.

I won't tell you anything about that night. I want to save it for the end. But the next morning I went to Archy's house. His mother said he'd gone to bed without supper and had not been seen since.

"He was terribly nervous and unhappy," she said.

I woke him up. He stood up dazedly, and then wilted as he remembered what had happened. He started toward the window, then stopped as though unwilling to look upon the wreckage of the basin.

"Tell me the worst," he said glumly.

"I've got a message from some of the Yacht Club members," I said. "You're being offered an honorary membership in the club."

"I don't think you're very funny," he said. "Are all the boats sunk?"

"Only Mr. Steele's. It was blown ashore after he left it across the bay. He's probably telephoning the insurance company now."

Archy looked at me strangely. "Am I crazy or you?"

I laughed. "Brace yourself, my lad. The hurricane switched course at the last moment. It struck to the north of us. The wind hit us from the land. So every craft was safe here in the lee. If you hadn't bottled them up, they'd all have been across the bay—and sunk. And the skippers are plenty grateful."

Archy threw open the shutters. Every boat was riding securely at its mooring. Every boat except the *Crazy Lady*, whose mast reared up mutely from the breakwater entrance. A sudden smile split Archy's face from ear to ear.

"I couldn't have wanted a better end for her," he said.

———

Paschall N. Strong

Puzzled

When asked to look after their house and pets by neighbors who were going away on holiday, the Joneses readily agreed. They duly looked after the dog, but they completely forgot about feeding the rabbit until one day the dog brought it in, dead, muddy, and bloody.

Full of remorse, the Joneses cleaned up the rabbit and put it in the cage, so that it would appear to have died a natural death.

When the neighbors returned, the Joneses received a rather puzzled telephone call from them. They said the rabbit had died the day before they left for their holiday, "and we buried him in the garden."

Nigel Rees

A Little Push

For many months the huge ship had been under construction. Now, she was finished and ready to launch. Her deck was polished and gleaming. The crew, in its starched white uniforms stood at the rail and saluted as her flags were raised to the top of the mast. The entire city had gathered on the dock to watch the ship be launched and slide down the slip into the bay.

At the moment of the scheduled launch, the giant blocks were removed, and everybody held their breath . . . but nothing happened. The big ship did not move. No one could figure out what to do. The captain scratched his head, and the crew remained at attention. Still, for several minutes, nothing happened. The ship didn't budge.

Finally, from the middle of the crowd, a tiny boy escaped from his mother and ran down the dock. He reached out his tiny hand and put it on the bow of the massive ship. Then he gave it a push with all the might his little body could muster.

All the people laughed at the comical sight. The idea of a small boy pushing a ship as big as a city was ludicrous. Then the whole crowd suddenly caught their breath as the huge ship groaned and slowly began to slide down the slip. When the ship splashed into the bay, a mighty cheer went up from the crowd—not for the ship, but for the little boy who had given it a push.

———

Written with facts from public records

Who's Listening?

Comedian Ted Ray was being installed as the president of the Variety Performers' Club, similar to the American Toastmasters Club. Part of his duties included saying grace before the banquet, a task to which he was not accustomed and which he performed in an inaudible mumble.

The toastmaster, in a typically stentorian tone, admonished Ray, "Speak up, sir, your guests can't hear you!"

Quick as a flash, Ray replied, "You mind your own business. I'm not talking to them."

Bernard Braden

Waiting to Be Asked

When much younger, I was supporting two children, but I was ill, and there was no money left for the expensive medication I needed. I resigned myself to putting up with the problem and continuing to work.

Also, I wanted to buy nicer clothes to angle for a better freelance writing job, but there was no money for that either. (I was a freelance office manager for a very small publisher who operated out of a relief organization's spare cubicle. On the side I wrote for religious publications that also operated on a shoestring.) I began praying hard for help.

The following week, after I started to pray seriously for help with these problems, my doctor's secretary called and said, "Another patient, a well-to-do woman, bought the medication you need but decided to have an operation instead. She gave us the medication and asked us to give it to someone who needed it but couldn't afford it. Come up here and get it and start taking it soon."

Shortly afterward, the head of the relief organization

came to me and said, "You're petite. You work hard. I want you to have first pick at this."

"This" turned out to be a big bag of fashionable clothes in my size. Apparently, a judge's wife had had her clothes stolen in a robbery. She had received an insurance settlement and bought all new clothes. The police later found her stolen clothes in a criminal's stash and had given them back to her. She decided to give them away, and of course, she gave them to the relief organization to distribute as they saw fit.

I recovered physically, and I got a better job, too. I started as a freelance proofreader at a publishing house and worked my way up to development editor over the next six years. My prayers had been answered.

I know that prayer is never magic, and we must accept suffering in many cases, but I am always amazed that we don't pray more often than we do about our true needs. Sometimes God seems only to be waiting to be asked.

——

Denyse O'Leary

The Bridge

Friendship is the bridge
between lonely and loved,
between a glance and a gaze.
It stretches from the fog into the sunshine,
from hopelessness into faith.
Friendship spans the gulf
between despair and joy,
between girl and boy.
It crosses the chasm from hell to heaven,
from God to man,
and from you to me.

———

Mary Hollingsworth
Just Between Friends

Doug's Light

✞

$\mathcal{D}$oug McKnight was a tall, handsome young man. He and his pretty wife, Pam, were in my class at the Christian university we attended in West Texas. After graduation, Doug and Pam started out successfully in business and in their marriage. After a few years, Doug was vice president of a large oil corporation, and Pam was building a dynamic interior decorating business. They also had beautiful, twelve-year-old twin daughters, Tara and Shannon. Life was good.

Then it happened. Doug was struck down by multiple sclerosis (MS). He went from the executive chair to a wheelchair in a very short time. And over the next seventeen years, Doug, Pam, and their girls struggled to cope with Doug's disease and the financial strain it created. Life was tough.

In the midst of Doug's MS, an interesting thing began to happen. Doug started finding ways to minister to other people from his wheelchair. Using his home computer, the telephone, his special van with a chairlift, and the U.S. Mail, Doug organized over four hundred volunteers at our church

to grade and mail World Bible School (WBS) correspon-
dence lessons and Bibles all over the world. Under his direction, the WBS volunteers could document over eighteen
hundred people who became Christians as a direct result of
their work. They sent the Light around the world.

My favorite memory of Doug, though, is about pizza.
Confined to his home much of the time due to his MS,
Doug often ordered pizza to be delivered for lunch. Over a
couple of years, he got to know the pizza delivery girl very
well. At one point, she even came to their house to study the
Bible with them at Doug's invitation.

One day Doug's daughter Tara was at home when the
noon pizza arrived. Having been a waitress herself, she
noticed that Doug didn't give a tip to the delivery girl, and
she chastised him about it. Doug just had not realized he
should tip the delivery person. So, because Doug was so
intent on doing the right thing in his life, he calculated from
his checkbook how many times over the past two years he
had ordered pizza and what the tip would have been. Then
the next time the delivery girl came, he gave her a seventy-
five-dollar tip! Can you imagine her reaction? His light, once
again, shone brightly.

Doug also decided he should be more active in sharing his
own personal testimony about the grace of God. So he
wrote his testimony into a letter format and ran off copies
on the photocopier. Then he folded the letters and put them
in envelopes, which he kept with him in his wheelchair.

When he met people who he thought might need to know Christ, Doug gave them copies of his testimony and asked them to read it. Many did and saw the light of God.

We lost Doug a little over a year ago. God finally called him home to peace and reward. But everyone who knew Doug was touched by the beacon of light from his soul. Doug's wheelchair, which most people would have considered a prison of darkness, became his prism of light to the lost. It helped him to refract the light of God into all its beautiful spectrum of colors and into the lives of people around him. This was Doug's light.

Hang On, Brother!

✦

We should have stopped sailing when we originally planned. But it was so easy to forget our worries on the sparkling Pacific, and we both needed an afternoon's escape.

Pepperdine University had been going through some difficult times. We had recently opened our new Malibu Beach campus, and we had kept our old one going in Los Angeles near the Watts area. Now we were beginning to wonder if we could operate both successfully. We had money problems, administrative problems, problems everywhere. So I was glad when my friend, Bill Banowsky, our university president, suggested we take out the fourteen-foot catamaran.

Near sunset we came back to shore, beached the catamaran, and returned to our driftwood fire. Over the darkening Pacific, the wind was picking up. Bill looked at me, a glint in his eyes, and I knew what he had in mind.

"Great!" I said. "One more time."

Together we began to push the light craft down the sand toward the water. The catamaran is a cat-rigged sailboat composed of two long metal pontoons, which support a raised deck of canvas capable of holding two or three people. Because of its unique design, the craft slices through the water with exceptional speed and power.

As we slid the boat into the water, I was pushing on the starboard side, and Bill was standing at the stern. The surf foamed at our waists, and we prepared to hoist ourselves onto the canvas deck.

Suddenly the wind caught the sail and snapped it with the sound of a rifle crack. The boat shot forward like a bullet. I managed to grab the stern of the starboard pontoon and was instantly yanked off my feet. I found myself being dragged out to sea.

Bill lunged forward, trying to catch the boat, but he was left behind. The last I saw of him was his shocked face as he screamed, "Climb on!" But, as the craft surged out to sea, I felt as if I were being dragged behind a runaway locomotive. I unsuccessfully tried to climb on board. Now it was too late to let go because the distance to shore was far greater than my swimming endurance.

As I was dragged along, the powerful water pressure pulled my pants off right over my shoes. I hung on, arms stretched before me, trying to keep my head above water. The ocean was icy, and my body was quickly becoming numb.

I tried to pull myself up on the pontoon, but try as I might, I couldn't lift myself even six inches. The racing water held me down and back. Panic filled me. This mindless craft would race on endlessly, towing me like some infuriated whale.

I tried to climb onto the pontoon again but fell back gasping. My arms were weakening, pain shot through my elbows and shoulders. How long could I hang on?

Alone under the darkening sky with only the roar of foaming water in my ears, I knew I faced death. *How ironic,* I thought, *when only minutes before I had been warming myself contentedly by the beach fire and discussing the university's problems with Bill.*

My thoughts turned to Helen and our four children. "Oh, God, help me, help me!" I gasped. "Give me strength to hang on."

My arms were like wood. I couldn't feel through my hands anymore. Once more. Just once more. I called on my last remaining strength and threw a leg over the pontoon. Pain seared through me as the back of my knee struck a sharp metal projection, and blood ran down my leg. I slipped back deeper into the churning water, coughing and choking.

I was now at least two miles from shore. Even if a search was sent out, I despaired of anyone finding me in that vast ocean. Soon my hands would slip from the cold metal pontoon, and I would sink into the ocean depths, like a sailor buried at sea.

Now the waves increased in size, and I lost all hope as the cold, foaming breakers crashed down on me. So many times, as a minister, I had told others that "God is our protection and our strength. He always helps in times of trouble" (Psalm 46:1, NCV), but now my faith was weak, and I was terrified.

"Oh, God, help me, help me," I continued praying as the surging catamaran pitched in the rolling waves. Over and over those words flooded my heart.

Then, as if prompted by something deep within me, my panicky feeling suddenly evaporated, leaving me able to study my enemy, the ocean waves. Until now, I had not been able to conquer my fear long enough to really look at how to combat it. I saw now that each time the bow of the catamaran rose to meet a big wave, my end of the pontoon was momentarily buried in the water.

I awaited my opportunity. Here came another wave . . . there! I had managed to hoist my leg over the pontoon.

Now wait. Here came another green, crashing roller. Quick, lift!

By using the waves, I had been able to shift more of my body out of the water. With each wave I was able to get more of me onto the pontoon. To my spent energy, God had added his power. Finally I lay on top of the boat's surface, hugging the cold metal, breathing hard. I looked up. The twenty-five-mile-per-hour wind was still driving us out to sea. It would be impossible to crawl forward to the tiller, but I could reach the rod guiding the rudder!

I shoved it as hard as I could, forcing the craft to turn toward shore. As she came about, the wind caught the sail with such enormous force that the boat capsized. But at least she was now dead in the water. I rolled onto the flat side of the exposed pontoon and lay there exhausted. "Thank you, God," I kept saying with every breath.

After a while I heard a faint voice calling: "Hang on, brother! Hang on!"

Bill and his son had commandeered a neighbor's boat and had come out to rescue me. I lay on the deck as we returned to shore; I was shivering cold, but my heart was singing songs of praise.

———

M. Norvel Young
former Chancellor Emeritus
of Pepperdine University

The Candy Train

The house on Caddo Street in Greenville, Texas, where I grew up was only one long block from the railroad track. Every night I went to sleep to the familiar sound of the 10:05 chugging past. And every morning I awoke to the 6:30 express and its long, steady blast as it sped along.

The street that ran beside our house came to a dead end at the railroad. And at the end of that block, next to the railroad, was a house that sat up on a small hill. As kids we loved to ride our bikes flying down that street toward the railroad and then up the steep driveway at the end, which slowed us down again. Then we'd race down the driveway and back up the street where we would turn around and do it all again. And again. We must have done it a thousand times over the years.

Charlie Johnson, the old man who lived in the house next to the railroad, was also the engineer on the train that came through our neighborhood every day at four o'clock. To us he was Uncle Charlie. So every day after school at four o'clock, we all raced our bikes down the street and up the hill into Uncle Charlie's yard.

When the train was about two blocks away, Uncle Charlie blew the train whistle two short and one long blast, which was his signal to his wife, who we called Aunt Martha. When she heard the signal, Aunt Martha came out into the yard with us to wave at Uncle Charlie and throw him a kiss as he went by.

Uncle Charlie was special to us for another reason. Every day he threw candy out the train window to the kids in his own yard. Sometimes there were little prizes among the pieces of candy. He always blew the whistle and laughed as we scrambled for the treats. And we all cheered and waved at him.

We called it the Candy Train. You can imagine why it's one of my favorite childhood memories. It was like seeing Santa Claus at the end of the parade every day of the year.

The Waving Girl

$\mathcal{T}$he young seaman watched the fading lights of Savannah as the freighter made its way slowly through the river toward the Atlantic. Although excited about his first trip aboard an oceangoing ship, he was already feeling homesick as he pulled up the collar of his jacket against the stiff breeze and peered into the blackness ahead. He shivered and moved away from the rail. His duties on deck were done, and he began making his way down to his quarters.

A husky boatswain met him at the bottom of the ladder. "Hold it, lad. Where do you think you're going?"

The boy bit his lip nervously. "I'm off duty now, sir. I was just going to turn in."

The man's eyes searched the boy's face and took note of his drooping shoulders. "Now that would be awfully rude of a young fellow, wouldn't it?" he asked.

He clamped a callused hand on the youngster's shoulder and turned him around. "There's a young lady to see you off," he said. "You don't want to miss her farewell, do you?"

Startled and afraid to argue, the young man stumbled back

up the ladder. *The boatswain must be playing a joke of some kind on him,* he thought. Being from the hill country of north Georgia, the boy knew no one in Savannah. Besides, they were away from the city now, and it was pitch black outside.

The older man marched him along the deck to the starboard side of the ship. The light from the Elba lighthouse shone ahead of them. The man stopped, leaned against the railing, and nodded toward the lighthouse. "She'll be waiting up there to give you a send-off."

The boy stared at him. "Who?" he croaked. "Who is going to be out there in the middle of the night? And how could I see her, even if she was?"

"You won't be able to see her," replied the boatswain, "but you'll see her lantern. She'll be standing on the porch of the lightkeeper's cottage swinging her lamp. Just keep watching."

Still expecting some joke, the seaman stared at the darker landmass on the horizon below the beacon light. *Was that a flicker of light near the shoreline? Or was it his imagination? No. It was a lantern swinging in the darkness!*

The boy jumped in startled surprise at a sudden blast of the ship's whistle.

"What was that for?" he asked.

The boatswain nodded toward the bobbing light. "We're answering her greeting," he replied.

"Who is she?"

The older sailor pulled his collar up against the chill and hunched over the railing. "I've heard her name, but I don't recall it. We just call her 'The Waving Girl.' They say her fiancé was a sailor, and when his ship left Savannah, she promised him she would greet every ship that entered and left the port until he got home."

He stuffed his hands in his pockets and glanced at the boy. "Kind of sad, though. She's been keeping her promise for years and years, but he's never come back."

They watched in silence as the light slowly disappeared. The boy tried to sort out his feelings. It had felt good to see the waving light and know that someone cared enough to bid them farewell in the middle of a dark, cold night, but the story behind her actions saddened him.

"Do you think it's true about her fiancé?"

The man grinned. "I don't know, lad. That's the story everyone tells about her. Maybe it's true, or maybe it's just a legend. Every sailor that leaves this port counts on seeing her wave a big white cloth in the daytime or her lantern at night. I've never heard of her missing a single passing ship."

They bade one another good-night, and the boy started briskly down the ladder. His shoulders no longer drooped, and he whistled a gentle tune.

On the shore, Florence Martus dimmed her lantern and set it by the door of the cottage where she lived with her brother, who kept the lights on the Savannah River. She wondered briefly about the men on the ship that had just passed. Were they lonely? Perhaps her greeting had lifted some sailor's spirits.

She slipped out of her warm robe and slippers and slid between the covers of her bed. A smile crossed her face as she thought of the romantic legend the sailors and the people of Savannah were telling about her. She had tried once to explain her faithfulness in greeting and bidding farewell to the ships.

"It's lonely on the island for a girl, so I started to wave at ships which passed. They began to return the greeting, and now they watch for me."

There is a statue erected to her, which says this:

HER IMMORTALITY STEMS FROM HER FRIENDLY GREETING
TO PASSING SHIPS,
A WELCOME TO STRANGERS ENTERING THE PORT
AND A FAREWELL TO WAVE THEM SAFELY ONWARD.

For forty-four years Florence Martus—The Waving Girl— kept her vigil. When her brother retired as lightkeeper in 1931, she was a celebrity among seamen from around the world—a simple girl overcoming her own loneliness by reaching out to cheer others.

———

A legend retold from public facts

Three Yellow Roses

$\mathcal{I}$ walked into the grocery store not particularly interested in buying groceries. I wasn't hungry. The pain of losing my husband of thirty-seven years was still too raw. And this grocery store held so many sweet memories.

Rudy often came with me, and almost every time he'd pretend to go off and look for something special. I knew what he was up to. I'd always spot him walking down the aisle with the three yellow roses in his hands. Rudy knew I loved yellow roses. With a heart filled with grief, I only wanted to buy my few items and leave, but even grocery shopping was different since Rudy had passed on. Shopping for one took time, a little more thought than it had for two.

Standing by the meat, I searched for the perfect small steak and remembered how Rudy had loved his steak.

Suddenly a woman came up beside me. She was blond, slim, and lovely in a soft green pantsuit. I watched as she picked up a large pack of T-bones, dropped them in her basket, hesitated, and then put them back. She turned to go and once again reached for the pack of steaks.

She saw me watching her and she smiled. "My husband loves T-bones, but honestly, at these prices, I don't know."

I swallowed the emotion down my throat and met her pale blue eyes. "My husband passed away eight days ago," I told her.

Glancing at the package in her hands, I fought to control the tremble in my voice. "Buy him the steaks. And cherish every moment you have together."

She nodded her head, and I saw the emotion in her eyes as she placed the package in her basket and wheeled away.

I turned and pushed my cart across the length of the store to the dairy products. There I stood, trying to decide which size milk I should buy. A quart, I finally decided and moved on to the ice-cream section near the front of the store. If nothing else, I could always fix myself an ice-cream cone. I placed the ice cream in my cart and looked down the aisle toward the produce.

I saw first the green suit, then recognized the pretty lady coming toward me. In her arms she carried a package. On her face was the brightest smile I had ever seen. I would swear a soft halo encircled her blond hair as she kept walking toward me, her eyes holding mine. As she came closer, I saw what she held and tears began misting in my eyes.

"These are for you," she said and placed three beautiful long-stemmed yellow roses in my arms. "When you go through the line, they will know these are paid for." She leaned over and placed a gentle kiss on my cheek, then smiled again.

I wanted to tell her what she'd done, what the roses meant, but still unable to speak, I watched as she walked away and tears clouded my vision. I looked down at the beautiful roses nestled in the green tissue wrapping and found it almost unreal. How did she know? Suddenly the answer seemed so clear: I wasn't alone.

"Oh, Rudy, you haven't forgotten me, have you?" I whispered, with the tears in my eyes. He was still with me, and she was his angel.

———

Author Unknown

The Hand

My daughter, Kathleen, was fifteen—too young to date seriously, but she had a boyfriend. One evening, when I was leaving to pick up my son, Paul, from baseball practice, she asked if she could just go with her boyfriend to pick up his little brother at a friend's house. She said they would come right back. I said, "All right, just make sure you wear your seat belt, and come right home."

It was my father's birthday and my three-year-old daughter, Therese, was already at my father's house waiting for us to come over with the cake I had yet to pick up at the store. I left to pick Paul up at school but decided to take the highway, rather than the shortcut along the back roads.

After leaving the school, Paul and I ran into the store for the cake and some last-minute goodies. As we were getting into the car, we heard and saw paramedics, fire trucks, three ambulances, and a multitude of police cars. I got a sick feeling in my stomach and said to Paul, "Somebody needs our prayers, quick." I wondered if there was a fire or a bad car accident. At one of the intersections I had to stop to let more emergency vehicles through and prayed, "Lord, those people need you right now, go to them, and place your protective hand over them."

We stopped at my parents' house to drop off the food, before going home to pick up Kathleen, but my father met me at the car and told us not to rush, the party could wait a bit, because Therese had fallen asleep.

"Which way did you go to the school?" he asked. "Because there was a bad accident on the back road, I heard someone was killed. It happened just about the time you had to pick up Paul at the school, and I know you always go that way. I was so happy to see you pull in; where's Kathleen?" I explained I was going back home to get her.

As I drove the short distance home, I couldn't help but worry: *What if she was involved in the accident?* I ran into the house and called out her name. Dead silence. Then the phone rang. It was her friend's mother, who worked in the emergency room of our local hospital. She only told me that that Kathleen and two boys were in an accident and were being transported to the hospital. I didn't call my husband at work, nor my parents; I just ran out the door.

At the hospital room, I could hear one of the paramedics softly talking to another parent there, saying, "I'm so sorry, so very sorry." I rushed by him and found the doctor in the hallway. He looked at me and asked if I believed in God, and with that my knees gave way.

I wasn't ready to accept the fact that Kathleen might be . . . "Oh, please, not my girl."

"No," he said, "you don't understand, do you believe in divine intervention?"

I stammered a weak, "Yes." Not having a clue what he was talking about.

He smiled at me and asked, "Do you know what shirt your daughter is wearing tonight?"

Shaking my head no, he told me to go down the hall and look. "Your daughter is blessed with angels, and so are you."

From what the emergency personnel told me, there is no way that my daughter should be alive, let alone only have a few scratches. Kathleen was lying on a cart, waiting for more x-rays. When I got to her, we both sobbed. As I was hugging her, I had the urge to check her shirt. Unzipping her jacket I read the words, "Jesus Saves."

I knew then what the doctor had meant. All three were treated and released. On the way home that night Kathleen told this story: "It was really weird, about a quarter of a mile before the accident, I said, 'Wait, we forgot to put our seat belts on; my mother will kill me.' Then a car was coming toward us in our lane. He swerved, and I knew we got hit in the passenger side of the car where I was sitting. We got hit a total of three times because the car kept spinning in a circle. I felt his little brother's hand on my shoulder, holding me tightly in place. But, Mom, after it was all over, I could still feel the hand on my shoulder. I looked and his little brother had flown out the back window of the car, as we later found out, on the first spin. It was an angel, Mom, I know it!"

I knew it too, especially when we went the next day to look at the car. It had been split in half, right underneath my daughter's seat. The driver of the other car, witnesses said, must have been traveling between ninety to ninety-five miles per hour, and the point of impact was directly at Kathleen's door. The police report stated that the car door was found fifty feet away from the accident scene, with the seat belt attached. So when the door broke loose, "the hand" was the only thing that saved my daughter's life.

God knew, long before I did, that my child was in trouble, and I will always thank Him for saving her life and restoring mine.

———

Story submitted by Worldwide Church of God

Is Your Hut Burning?

The only survivor of a shipwreck was washed up on a small, uninhabited island. He prayed feverishly for God to rescue him, and every day he scanned the horizon for help, but none seemed forthcoming. Exhausted, he eventually managed to build a little hut out of driftwood for protection from the elements and to store his few possessions. But then one day, after scavenging for food, he arrived home to find his little hut in flames, the smoke rolling up to the sky. The worst had happened; everything was lost.

He was stunned with grief and anger. "God, how could you do this to me?" he cried.

Early the next day, however, he was awakened by the sound of a ship that was approaching the island. It had come to rescue him.

"How did you know I was here?" the weary man asked his rescuers.

"We saw your smoke signal," they replied.

It's easy to get discouraged when things are going bad. But we shouldn't lose heart, because God is at work in our lives, even in the midst of pain and suffering. Remember, next time your little hut is burning to the ground—it just may be a smoke signal that summons the grace of God.

———

Author Unknown

The Day I Met Daniel

$\mathcal{I}$t was an unusually cold day for the month of May. Spring had arrived, and everything was alive with color. But a cold front from the north had brought winter's chill back to Indiana. I sat with two friends in the picture window of a quaint restaurant just off the corner of the town square. The food and the company were both especially good that day. As we talked, my attention was drawn outside, across the street. There, walking into town, was a man who appeared to be carrying all his worldly goods on his back. He was carrying a well-worn sign that read, "I will work for food."

My heart sank. I brought him to the attention of my friends and noticed that others around us had stopped eating to focus on him. Heads moved in a mixture of sadness and disbelief. We continued with our meal, but his image lingered in my mind.

We finished our meal and went our separate ways. I had errands to do and quickly set out to accomplish them. I glanced toward the town square, looking somewhat half-heartedly for the strange visitor. I was fearful, knowing that

137

seeing him again would call for some response. I drove through town and saw nothing of him. I made some purchases at a store and got back in my car. Deep within me, the Spirit of God kept speaking to me: "Don't go back to the office until you've at least driven once more around the square."

And so, with some hesitancy, I headed back into town. As I turned the square's third corner, I saw him. He was standing on the steps of the storefront church, going though his sack. I stopped and looked, feeling both compelled to speak to him, yet wanting to drive on. The empty parking space on the corner seemed to be a sign from God—an invitation to park.

I pulled in, got out, and approached the town's newest visitor.

"Looking for the pastor?" I asked.

"Not really," he replied. "Just resting."

"Have you eaten today?"

"Oh, I ate something early this morning."

"Would you like to have lunch with me?"

"Do you have some work I could do for you?"

"No work," I replied. "I commute here to work from the city, but I would like to take you to lunch."

"Sure," he replied with a smile.

As he began to gather his things, I asked some surface questions. "Where you headed?"

"St. Louis."

"Where you from?"

"Oh, all over, mostly Florida."

"How long you been walking?"

"Fourteen years," came the reply.

I knew I had met someone unusual. We sat across from each other in the same restaurant I had left earlier. His face was weathered slightly beyond his thirty-eight years. His eyes were dark yet clear, and he spoke with an eloquence and articulation that was startling. He removed his jacket to reveal a bright red T-shirt that said, "Jesus Is the Never-Ending Story."

Then Daniel's story began to unfold. He had seen rough times early in life. He'd made some wrong choices and reaped the consequences. Fourteen years earlier, while backpacking across the country, he had stopped on the beach in Daytona. He tried to hire on with some men who were putting up a large tent and some equipment. A concert, he thought. He was hired, but the tent would not house a concert but revival services, and in those services he saw life more clearly. He gave his life to God.

"Nothing's been the same since," he said. "I felt the Lord telling me to keep walking, and so I did, some fourteen years now."

"Ever think of stopping?" I asked.

"Oh, once in a while, when it seems to get the best of me. But God has given me this calling. I give out Bibles. That's what's in my sack. I work to buy food and Bibles, and I give them out when His Spirit leads."

I sat amazed. My homeless friend was not homeless. He

was on a mission and lived this way by choice. The question burned inside for a moment and then I asked: "What's it like?"

"What?"

"To walk into a town carrying all your things on your back and to show your sign?"

"Oh, it was humiliating at first. People would stare and make comments. Once someone tossed a piece of half-eaten bread and made a gesture that certainly didn't make me feel welcome. But then it became humbling to realize that God was using me to touch lives and change people's concepts of other folks like me."

My concept was changing too. We finished our dessert and gathered his things. Just outside the door, he paused. He turned to me and said, "Come ye blessed of my Father and inherit the kingdom I've prepared for you. For when I was hungry you gave me food, when I was thirsty you gave me drink, a stranger and you took me in."

I felt as if we were on holy ground. "Could you use another Bible?" I asked.

He said he preferred a certain translation. It traveled well and was not too heavy. It was also his personal favorite. "I've read through it fourteen times," he said.

"I'm not sure we've got one of those, but let's stop by our church and see." I was able to find my new friend a Bible that would do well, and he seemed very grateful. "Where you headed from here?"

"Well, I found this little map on the back of this amuse-ment park coupon."

"Are you hoping to hire on there for a while?"

"No, I just figure I should go there. I figure someone under that star right there needs a Bible, so that's where I'm going next."

He smiled, and the warmth of his spirit radiated the sin-cerity of his mission. I drove him back to the town square where we'd met two hours earlier, and as we drove, it started raining. We parked and unloaded his things.

"Would you sign my autograph book?" he asked. "I like to keep messages from folks I meet."

I wrote in his little book that his commitment to his call-ing had touched my life. I encouraged him to stay strong. And I left him with a verse of scripture, in Jeremiah: "'I know the plans I have for you,' declares the LORD, 'plans to prosper you and not to harm you, plans to give you hope and a future.'"

"Thanks, man," he said. "I know we just met and we're really just strangers, but I love you."

"I know," I said. "I love you too."

"The Lord is good."

"Yes, He is. How long has it been since someone hugged you?" I asked.

"A long time," he replied.

And so on the busy street corner in the drizzling rain, my new friend and I embraced, and I felt deep inside that I had been changed. He put his things on his back, smiled his winning smile, and said, "See you in the New Jerusalem."

"I'll be there!" was my reply.

He began his journey again. He headed away with his sign dangling from his bedroll and pack of Bibles. He stopped, turned, and said, "When you see something that makes you think of me, will you pray for me?"

"You bet," I shouted back, "God bless."

"God bless."

And that was the last I saw him. Late that evening as I left my office, the wind blew strong. The cold front had settled hard upon the town. I bundled up and hurried to my car. As I sat back and reached for the emergency brake, I saw them—a pair of well-worn brown work gloves neatly laid over the length of the handle. I picked them up and thought of my friend and wondered if his hands would stay warm that night without them. I remembered his words: "If you see something that makes you think of me, will you pray for me?"

Today his gloves lie on the desk in my office. They help me to see the world and its people in a new way, and they help me remember those two hours with my unique friend and to pray for his ministry.

"See you in the New Jerusalem," he said.

Yes, Daniel, I know I will.

———

Author Unknown

What Would Jesus Do?

❧

*C*hances are, you've seen kids in your church wearing bracelets with the initials WWJD, which stands for "What Would Jesus Do?"

Well, I've seen them too, but it was only recently that I learned the exciting story behind the bracelets.

It began a century ago, when a minister named Charles Sheldon wrote a novel called *In His Steps*. The setting is an ordinary city called Raymond, and one Sunday morning Henry Maxwell was preaching a sermon about how to follow Christ's example of sacrificial love.

The service was suddenly interrupted as a tramp stood up and walked to the front of the sanctuary. He had been out of work for a year, he stated, yet not a single person in Raymond had helped him find another job, not even Brother Maxwell.

Twisting his shabby hat in his hands, the tramp said, "I was wondering if what you call following Jesus is the same thing as what He taught. What do you mean when you sing, 'I'll go with Him, with Him, all the way?' I get puzzled," the tramp continued, "when I see so many Christians living in luxury and remembering how my wife died in a tenement. A member of this church was the owner of that tenement. It seems there's an awful lot of trouble in the world that somehow wouldn't exist if all the people who sing such songs went and lived them out. I suppose I don't understand. But what would Jesus do?"

At that point the tramp sat down.

The following Sunday, the minister made a stunning proposal. He was looking for volunteers willing to pledge themselves for an entire year to do nothing without first asking the question, "What would Jesus do?" The volunteers must then do exactly that, no matter what the consequences. Some fifty people made the pledge, and almost at once, a remarkable series of events began to take place.

The editor of the local newspaper had been accepting lucrative ads from the local saloons. Would Jesus do this? No, he decided, and canceled the ads.

A young singer gave up a promising career on the stage in order to sing at tent meetings on Skid Row. A young heiress took in a homeless woman, to the horror of her fashionable family. A businessman decided that Jesus wanted him to make his tenements as warm and comfortable as his own home.

A few years ago, a youth leader in Holland, Michigan, was so inspired by this classic that she had bracelets made bearing the letters WWJD and gave them to kids in the church. The idea caught fire, and today millions of kids wear them.

If your kids are among them, ask them if they know the story behind the bracelets. If they don't, give them a copy of *In His Steps*. It's a book millions have enjoyed over the century.

Long after they've given up wearing the bracelets, through all the trials and temptations of life, it may inspire your kids to ask that one, quiet question: "What Would Jesus Do?"

———

Sidney Colson

The Gift of Hope

$\mathcal{I}$ am a mother of three and have recently completed my college degree.

The last class I had to take was sociology. The teacher was absolutely inspiring, having the qualities I wish every human being had been graced with. Her last project of the term was called "Smile."

The class was asked to go out and smile at three people and document their reactions. I am a very friendly person and always smile at everyone and say hello anyway, so I thought, this would be a piece of cake.

Soon after we were assigned the project, my husband, youngest son, and I went out to McDonald's one crisp March morning. It was just our way of sharing special playtime with our son. We were standing in line, waiting to be served, when all of a sudden everyone around us began to back away, and then even my husband did. I did not move an inch, an overwhelming feeling of panic welled up inside of me as I turned to see why they had moved.

As I turned around I smelled a horrible "dirty body"

smell, and there standing behind me, were two poor home-less men. As I looked down at the shorter gentleman close to me, he was smiling. His beautiful sky-blue eyes were full of God's light as he searched for acceptance. He said, "Good day" as he counted the few coins he had been clutching.

The second man fumbled with his hands as he stood behind his friend. I realized the second man was mentally deficient, and the blue-eyed gentleman was his salvation. I held my tears as I stood there with them.

The young lady at the counter asked him what they wanted. He said, "Coffee is all, Miss" because that was all they could afford. (If they wanted to sit in the restaurant, they had to buy something.)

Then I really felt it—the compulsion was so great I almost reached out and embraced the little man with the blue eyes. That is when I noticed all eyes in the restaurant were set on me, judging my every action.

I smiled and asked the young lady behind the counter to give me two more breakfast meals on a separate tray. I then walked around the corner to the table that the men had cho-sen as a resting spot. I put the tray on the table and laid my hand on the blue-eyed gentleman's cold hand.

He looked up at me, with tears in his eyes, and said, "Thank you."

I leaned over, began to pat his hand, and said, "I did not do this for you. God is here working through me to give you hope."

I started to cry as I walked away to join my husband and son. When I sat down my husband smiled at me and said, "That is why God gave you to me, honey. To give me hope."

We held hands for a moment, and at that time we knew that only because of the grace that we had been given were we able to give.

———

Author Unknown

Homecoming

While waiting to pick up a friend at the airport in Portland, Oregon, I had one of those life-changing experiences that you hear other people talk about—the kind that sneaks up on you unexpectedly.

This one occurred a mere two feet away from me.

Straining to locate my friend among the passengers deplaning through the jetway, I noticed a man coming toward me carrying two light bags. He stopped right next to me to greet his family.

First he motioned to his youngest son (maybe six years old) as he laid down his bags. They gave each other a long, loving hug. As they separated enough to look in each other's face, I heard the father say, "It's so good to see you, son. I missed you so much!" His son smiled somewhat shyly, averted his eyes and replied softly, "Me, too, Dad!"

Then the man stood up, gazed in the eyes of his oldest son (maybe nine or ten) and while cupping his son's face in his hands said, "You're already quite the young man. I love you very much, Zach!" They too hugged a most loving, tender hug.

While this was happening, a baby girl (perhaps one or one-and-a-half) was squirming excitedly in her mother's arms, never once taking her little eyes off the wonderful sight of her returning father. The man said, "Hi, baby girl!" as he gently took the child from her mother. He quickly kissed her face all over and then held her close to his chest while rocking her from side to side. The little girl instantly relaxed and simply laid her head on his shoulder, motionless in pure contentment.

After several moments, he handed his daughter to his oldest son and declared, "I've saved the best for last!" and proceeded to give his wife the longest, most passionate kiss I ever remember seeing. He gazed into her eyes for several seconds and then silently mouthed, "I love you so much!" They stared at each other's eyes, beaming big smiles at one another, while holding both hands.

For an instant they reminded me of newlyweds, but I knew by the age of their kids that they couldn't possibly be. I puzzled about it for a moment then realized how totally engrossed I was in the wonderful display of unconditional love not more than an arm's length away from me.

I suddenly felt uncomfortable, as if I was invading something sacred, but was amazed to hear my own voice nervously ask, "Wow! How long have you two been married?"

"Been together fourteen years total, married twelve of those," he replied, without breaking his gaze from his lovely wife's face.

"Well then, how long have you been away?" I asked.

The man finally turned and looked at me, still beaming his joyous smile. "Two whole days!"

Two days? I was stunned.

By the intensity of the greeting, I had assumed he'd been gone for at least several weeks—if not months. I know my expression betrayed me. I said almost offhandedly, hoping to end my intrusion with some semblance of grace (and to get back to searching for my friend), "I hope my marriage is still that passionate after twelve years!"

The man suddenly stopped smiling. He looked me straight in the eye, and with forcefulness that burned right into my soul, he told me something that left me a different person. He told me, "Don't hope, friend—decide!" Then he flashed me his wonderful smile again, shook my hand and said, "God bless!"

With that, he and his family turned and strode away together.

I was still watching that exceptional man and his special family walk just out of sight when my friend came up to me and asked, "What'cha looking at?"

Without hesitating, and with a curious sense of certainty, I replied, "My future!"

———

Carl Sandburg

The Legacy

𝒮ometimes when I read of great men leaving vast for-
tunes to their heirs, I smile to myself. My own dad was a
great man. Yet the legacy he left was not tangible "things." It
was far greater than jewels or wealth. The legacy my dad left
was the legacy of laughter.

I was born during the Depression, when times were not
just hard, they were almost impossible. We lived on a little
farm outside of a logging community in northwestern
Washington State. It was a sunup to sundown existence.
Mom trotted to get more done. Dad kept the farm and
worked every other job he could find, and there were precious few of them! We had enough to eat and wear, but at
times there wasn't even a postage stamp to send a letter—
and stamps only cost two cents. Some years they made fifty
dollars, if they were lucky, which went for salt, sugar, and
other things we couldn't raise.

It was grim and hard, no time for joy and gladness. Yet in
our home, the Depression was something for others. We
never considered ourselves poor; poor people had less than

we did! The difference was, we laughed. From early child-hood, no matter how bad things were, we laughed—cleans-ing, healing laughter, often chasing away the tears. We ended childhood arguments with a laugh. When we didn't have money to go places, we stayed home, did something else, and laughed.

The Depression ended, only to be followed by World War II. There wasn't much laughter in the world then. There was anguish, friends and loved ones in the service. Yet in spite of our sorrows, we still laughed. When there was no sugar for cookies and candy, Mom popped corn, or made "dough-gods," funny little pieces of dough fried directly on the well-scrubbed kitchen range. In winter we curled up by the light of kerosene lamps, reading our books. In summer we ran through the woods, played our games, and eventually flopped to the ground, to look at cloud pictures and laugh.

The day the war ended everyone laughed. People shouted, wildly making sure everyone knew the good news—we were free!

Years passed. There was more money for such things as camping trips, things that held families together. There were walks to the river, fishing trips, cookouts, all invisibly bind-ing us together with memories. Our laughter rang golden as the sunlight, warm as the campfires. We laughed at the dog, the cat, ourselves, each other. We laughed because we were alive. Season followed season; we still laughed.

My older brother became of service age during the Korean

conflict. He was fortunate. He was sent to Japan. He came home with funny tales of a different way of life, how he felt big and powerful next to the smaller Japanese race. We loved it all—and laughed.

As time passed and the boys married, the family scattered. Yet our family reunions were times of joy, gladness, and laughter.

About then a little eight-year-old boy came to live with Dad, Mom, and me. He was a solemn little fellow, all big eyes, who huddled close to Mom. Not for long. Dad taught him to laugh, just as the rest of us had been taught. Soon we were laughing at Jerry's antics, from getting stuck in the rain-barrel under the eaves to sliding off the snow-covered roof and landing upside-down in a snowbank.

Our biggest test was yet to come. Dad hadn't been feeling well. It was the summer of 1968. We took him to the hospital, teased him, and shaved him with a new electric razor on Saturday. Sunday night he took a turn for the worse and died the next morning quietly, as he had lived, with dignity.

The funeral was over, and by the time we reached home, the heavens were black. Wild storm clouds gathered; the rain poured. My two brothers and I stood numbly on the covered backporch, watching the storm, just as we had watched many storms before.

Bang! Crash! Boom! What a wild day it was! It snatched from me words I'd have held back if I'd only stopped to think. I looked up into those tumultuous heavens and said,

"Would you believe it? Dad's just gotten up there, and already he's throwing a big party!" My brothers stared. Then it came. Laughter louder than thunder, mingled with tears the size of the spattering raindrops. Dad's legacy to us—the laughter that would heal, console, and allow us to go on.

Years have passed, many of them. Yet when I stand watching a storm, for a moment I am back in the old homeplace, watching the storms of life as well as the weather. I am hearing again the hearty laughter of a dad who had learned to ride the swells of those storms.

He never made a lot of money. He never held a high office. He never claimed to be anything except what he was—a man who loved his family. But Dad's greatest gift to his children can never be lost.

What is the measure of a man except what he gives those who follow? They will inevitably find themselves influenced by those winding ruts he has created.

There are many things a man can leave his heirs, but few will ever match the legacy of laughter my dad gave his children.

———

Colleen L. Reece

Grandmother's Button Jar

It stands on the window shelf above my typewriter, next to the ceramic pot that holds my pencils and pens: a four-ounce clear glass jar that once held shapeless coffee granules. It's jammed with buttons of all shapes and sizes, each circle or square, each color a memory to warm the spirit.

I spill the contents in the sunlight onto my desk; as I spread and finger them, the buttons come to life. Each tells a story of my grandmother's marriage.

Carefully I turn the small delicate china pansy that my grandmother, after much searching, finally ordered from the catalog at the general store. The button matched the fabric of the dress she sewed for her first meeting with the man she would later marry.

At the Harvest Dance, when they were introduced, he said, "They match your eyes, those pretty flowers," and the warmth in his voice made her blush.

As I move the buttons on my desk, a tiny pearl glistens in the bright light. It was one of the closely spaced fastenings that trickled down the lace jacket of the wedding dress she fashioned and then stitched by hand because the fabric was too fragile to trust to her sewing machine.

There are from that jar many pale wee creatures in pastels. They fastened baby sweaters she knitted for each child as their family and their love grew.

She showed me each wooden button and described the sweaters and jackets they helped hold tight about small children; buttons bulky enough so that awkward little hands could manage them.

And, as the children grew, there were buttons of favorite colors to match the dresses she stitched throughout the years, because money was not plentiful, and her love gave her strength for the labor which she called her "creativity time."

My mother remembers how her mother sat at that sewing machine with children playing on the floor around her. In time, Grandfather bought her an electric machine, and she could speed through seams endlessly, it seemed, without tiring.

And on Easter, when she had sewn matching dresses in navy blue with bright red-and-white buttons marching down to their waists for all my aunts, photographers waiting at the town church to photograph the Easter Parade paid more attention to her family than they did to the local celebrities.

When many of her friends could afford furs, Grandmother knitted a full-length cape to wear to a town function. It resembled the skin of a mink, and she adorned it with amber buttons that perfectly matched the tint of the wool. She was the center of attention, winning the admiration of both men and women. And Granddad beamed at the compliments paid to her.

Each button in that jar had a place in her heart and in her memory, and she saved them carefully through the years, one button for each important event in her life.

I fondle the buttons and carefully place them back in the jar.

The last button is a brilliant crystal centered in lustrous onyx. It secured about her the mourning suit she sewed with trembling hands the week Grandfather waited for death. The sparkle of the button fulfilled a wish he had expressed that "you won't become a dull colorless woman after I've gone."

Sometime later she gave me the button jar. It's mine to pass on to my daughter, so she'll know the story of her great-grandmother.

I turn my grandmother's button jar on the shelf so that the sun will warm all the symbols of her life—so they'll come alive in its rays, bouncing sunlight into my eyes and keeping bright memories of my grandmother.

———

Naomi Cherkofsky

'Twarn't Me

'Twarn't me, 'twas the Lord.
I always told him, "I trust you.
I don't know where to go
or what to do,
but I expect you to lead me."
And he always did.

———

Harriet Tubman

God, Is That You?

$\mathcal{A}$ young man had been to Wednesday night Bible study, where the pastor talked about listening to God and obeying the Lord's voice. The young man couldn't help but wonder, *Does God still speak to people?* After the service he went out with some friends for coffee and pie, and they discussed the message. Several people told how God had led them in different ways.

Driving home from the restaurant, the young man prayed, "God, if You still speak to people, speak to me. I will listen. I will do my best to obey."

As he drove down the main street of his town, he had the strangest thought to stop and buy a gallon of milk. He shook his head and said out loud, "God, is that You?"

He didn't get a reply, so he drove on toward home. But again the thought came: *Buy a gallon of milk.* The young man thought about Samuel and how he didn't recognize the voice of God, and how little Samuel ran to Eli.

"Okay, God, in case that's You, I will buy the milk."

It didn't seem like too hard a test of obedience. He could

always use the milk. He stopped and bought a gallon of milk and started off toward home.

As he passed Seventh Street, something told him to turn down the street. This is crazy, he thought and drove on past the intersection. Again, he felt that he should turn down Seventh Street. At the next intersection, he turned back and headed down Seventh. Half jokingly, he said out loud, "Okay, God, I will."

He drove several blocks, when suddenly he felt that he should stop. He pulled over to the curb and looked around. It wasn't the best, but it wasn't the worst of neighborhoods either. All the businesses were closed, and most of the houses looked dark.

He sensed something say, "Go and give the milk to the people in the house across the street."

The young man looked at the house. No lights shone from its windows.

He started to open the door and then sat back in the car seat. "Lord, this is insane. Those people are asleep, and if I wake them up, they're going to be mad, and I will look stupid."

Again, he felt that he should go and give the milk. Finally, he opened the door, "Okay, God, if this is You, I will go to the door and give them the milk. But if they don't answer right away, I'm out of here."

He walked across the street and rang the bell. He could hear some noise inside. A man's voice yelled out, "Who is it? What do you want?"

The door opened before the young man could get away. A man stood there in his jeans and T-shirt. He had a strange look on his face, and he didn't seem too happy to have a stranger standing on his doorstep.

"What is it?"

The young man thrust out the gallon of milk. "Here, I brought this to you."

The man took the milk and rushed down a hallway speaking loudly in Spanish. From down the hall came a woman carrying the milk toward the kitchen. The man was following her holding a crying baby.

With tears streaming down his face, he said, "We were just praying. We had some big bills this month, and we ran out of money. We didn't have any milk for our baby. I was just praying and asking God to show me how to get some milk."

From the kitchen, his wife yelled out, "I asked Him to send an angel with some. Are you an angel?"

The young man reached into his wallet, pulled out all the money he had, and placed it in the man's hand. He turned and walked across the street toward his car, blinking back tears. He knew that God still answers prayers.

Author Unknown

The Teacher's Challenge

*A*s a new teacher entering my sixth grade classroom, I was soon greeted by those teachers who had preceded me with those same students. They gave me a very vivid description of what lay ahead for me. For the past five years each in turn had tried every known method to deal with an incorrigible boy whom I shall call Will. To cope with his behavior, teachers had deprived him of playground privileges, paddled him, sent him to the office, and expelled him. Others tried granting him special privileges such as allowing him to be one of the captains in choosing players for the spelling match or the ball team—anything to build self-esteem. My friends warned me that all their efforts had been in vain.

By my third day I realized that my teacher friends had not exaggerated. In the classroom he repeatedly yelled out as I talked; he tripped anyone who walked down the aisle. Often he would lie on the floor or throw erasers across the room and even become profane at times.

I had no success in dealing with him in the presence of his peers; so ours turned out to be a "one-on-one" affair. In these sessions he was always in a sullen pout, sometimes refusing to answer me, other times yelling at me. Little by little I sensed a bit of devotion to his mother. Also I noted that he was very proud of his pet rooster, Sambo. When my patience was almost exhausted, I reasoned that we all have a weak, vulnerable spot somewhere. It was then that I resolved to find Will's Achilles heel. Finally I inquired if I might visit his mother and likewise get to see Sambo. His consent was slow in coming, but finally he did agree.

Before my visit I learned that his irresponsible father was a truck driver who seldom came home, and neither did his paycheck. The mother was terminally ill with tuberculosis and the fifteen-year-old daughter had dropped out of school to care for the mother.

When I arrived at Will's home, I found a very dilapidated house with meager furnishings. In the absence of chairs I even sat on an apple crate. The poor bedridden mother was very weak yet thanked me for coming. Next I got to see Sambo. Will had trained him to crow so that he might be rewarded with a few grains of corn. Also he would stand on tiptoe, then fly upward to get a morsel of bread that Will held high above his head.

Although Will was somewhat sociable when I visited his home, the old sullen, obstinate attitude was still very prevalent in the classroom. In privacy I often inquired about his mother or asked if Sambo had learned any more tricks.

My visits continued, and I took food and various articles

to add to the mother's comfort. I even took seeds and a leg band for Sambo. I noticed a wee bit of improvement.

When school resumed following our Thanksgiving holidays, Will was at his worst, obnoxious to his classmates and completely ignoring me. At the close of that unbearable day when the children were going home, I plucked Will's sleeve and asked him to remain with me for a few minutes. Alone, I asked why he was so ugly today. I got no reply; instead he just stared, acting as if he could neither hear nor speak. Finally when I noticed that he was trembling, I laid my arm across his shoulders as he blurted out, "They killed Sambo so that we could have something to eat for Thanksgiving dinner."

The two of us sat on a bench side by side for a long time, my arm around his shoulders, with tears running down both our cheeks. Friends in loss. Friends at last.

———

India M. Allmon

From the Cherry Tree

J recall many incidents of the summer of 1887 that followed my soul's sudden awakening. I did nothing but explore with my hands and learn the name of every object that I touched; and the more I handled things and learned their names and uses, the more joyous and confident grew my sense of kinship with the rest of the world.

When the time of daisies and buttercups came, Miss Sullivan took me by the hand across the fields, where men were preparing the earth for the seed, to the banks of the Tennessee River, and there, sitting on the warm grass, I had my first lessons in nature. I learned how the sun and the rain make every tree grow out of the ground, how birds build their nests and live from land to land, how the squirrel, the deer, the lion, and every other creature finds food and shelter. As my knowledge of things grew, I felt more and more the delight of the world I was in. Long before I learned to do a sum in arithmetic or describe the shape of the earth, Miss Sullivan had taught me to find beauty in the fragrant woods, in every blade of grass, and in the curves and dimples of my baby sister's hand. She linked my earliest thoughts with nature and made me feel that birds and flowers and I were happy peers.

About this time I had an experience which taught me that nature is not always kind. One day my teacher and I were returning from a long walk. The morning had been fine, but it was growing warm when at last we turned our faces homeward. Two or three times we stopped to rest under a tree. Our last stop was under a wild cherry tree a short distance from the house. The shade was pleasant and the tree was so easy to climb that, with my teacher's assistance, I was able to scramble to a seat in the branches. It was so cool up in the tree that Miss Sullivan proposed that we have our lunch there. I promised to keep still while she went to the house to get our lunch.

Suddenly a change passed over the tree. All the sun's warmth left the air. I knew the sky was black, because all the heat, which meant light to me, had died out of the atmosphere. A strange odor came up from the earth; I knew what it was—it was the odor that always comes before a thunderstorm, and a nameless fear clutched at my heart. I felt absolutely alone, cut off from my friends and the firm earth. I remained still and a chilling terror crept over me. I longed for my teacher's return, but above all things, I wanted to get down from that tree.

There was a moment of silence, then a stirring of the leaves. A shiver ran through the tree, and the wind sent forth a blast that would have knocked me off had I not clung to the branch with all my might. The tree swayed and strained. The small twigs snapped and fell about me. A wild impulse to jump seized me, but terror held me fast. I crouched down in the fork of the tree. The branches lashed about me. Just as I was thinking the tree and I should fall together, my teacher seized my hand and helped me down. I clung to her, trembling with joy to feel the earth under my feet once more.

After this experience it was a long time before I climbed another tree.

———

Helen Keller

God's Wings

After a fire in Yellowstone National Forest, rangers began their trek up a mountain to assess the inferno's damage.

One ranger found a bird literally petrified in ashes, perched statuesquely on the ground at the base of a tree.

Somewhat sickened by the eerie sight, he tipped over the bird with a stick.

When he gently struck it, three tiny chicks scurried from under their dead mother's wings. The loving mother, keenly aware of impending disaster, had carried her offspring to the base of the tree and gathered them under her wings, instinctively knowing that the toxic smoke would rise. She could have flown to safety but had refused to abandon her babies. When the blaze had arrived and the heat had scorched her small body, the mother had remained steadfast.

Because she had been willing to die, those under the cover of her wings would live.

"He will cover you with his feathers, and under his wings you will find refuge." (Psalm 91:4)

———

Retold from facts in the public record

Lights Out

✦

*O*f all the bugle calls used in the United States armed services, none is more popular or better known than "Taps." Probably not one American in twenty has heard of how this famous call was first blown.

It happened in Virginia in July 1862. After seven days of bitter fighting before Richmond, the North's Army of the Potomac lay encamped at Harrison's Landing on the James River. Vacant places in the ranks were a sharp reminder of the heavy losses that had been suffered, and to officers and men alike, there now came a sobering realization of what a terrible toll the War between the States was sure to take before it was all over.

Up and down the long, winding valley rose the bugle calls, echoing to the distant hills. The rhythm of camp life was punctuated by these soaring notes. If it had not been for tents and uniforms, the setting would have suited a summer idyll.

Now, with time heavy on their hands, the thoughts of more than one soldier turned to home and loved ones in the

North. As nostalgia rested heavily on the troops, the close of each day found many men in a mood not untouched with sadness.

Some of this feeling must have crept into the consciousness of General Daniel Butterfield. A brave commander, he was also an expert musician, with ears keenly attuned to harmony. While homesickness pervaded the army and the nights were filled with tender retrospection, he took a sudden dislike to the discordant "Lights Out" call, which had been handed down from the early days of West Point.

All by himself, he began to turn over in his mind a combination of notes that would express the peacefulness of a great camp after nightfall—soldiers sleeping, sentries keeping watch under the stars, rest after labor. The scene must have inspired the musical phrases of "Taps."

When General Butterfield was satisfied with his musical combination, he sent for his brigade bugler, Oliver W. Norton. Whistling the notes over and over, he taught them to the young musician. Whenever Norton made a mistake, General Butterfield would correct him, and in a short time the bugler was able to blow "Taps" perfectly. In order to preserve the call, the general copied down the notes on the back of an old envelope.

That same night General Butterfield's brigade was the first to hear the lingering refrain. Its music carried up and down the valley, and the wistful, haunting notes struck a responsive chord with thousands of other listeners.

The next morning General Butterfield was besieged by the buglers of other camps. "Taps" had caught their fancy, and they were curious about it. They wanted to know its origin, its meaning, and even asked for a copy of the music. All were given permission to use it.

Whenever the "Taps" was blown among Union forces after that, it excited immediate interest. The music lingered in the memory, and every soldier came to love it. It passed from corps to corps until, at last, by general order, it was substituted for the old "Lights Out" call and was officially printed in the army regulations.

Since that time, "Taps" has become an American tradition. It is used for military burial services by veterans of all wars—undoubtedly its most poignant associations. It moves listeners as no other bugle call can, and at the first notes a hush will fall over the noisiest crowd.

Life was certainly kind to the call's composer. At the close of the war, General Butterfield entered business in New York, where, by reason of his great organizing ability, he was frequently called upon to take charge of public parades and exhibitions. When he finally retired, it was to a home at Cold Spring, New York, where just across the Hudson, he could hear the notes of his beloved "Taps" sounded every evening by the bugler at West Point.

Retold from facts in the public record

The Letter

In the shabby basement of an old house in Atlanta, Georgia, lived a young widow and her little girl. During the Civil War, she had married a young Confederate soldier, against her Yankee father's will, and had moved with him south, to Atlanta. Her wealthy father, angry and hurt at what he considered to be her disloyalty, both to him and the North, told her never to come back.

The soldier had died bravely during the war, and his death left his wife and child without any support. Alone in Atlanta, Margaret did washing, ironing, and other menial jobs that she could find to help her scrape by and feed little Anna. Their clothes became ragged, and they were both ill from sleeping in the damp, cold basement.

Anna loved to hear her mother's stories about her home in the North. She sat in her mother's lap and listened for hours to descriptions of the big, brick house in Boston, the sprawling shade trees, the beautiful flower gardens, and the wide grassy lawn. She loved to imagine the horses trotting across the meadow, the smell of bread baking in the kitchen, and the soft feel of the fourposter feather beds. Although Anna had never seen her mother's home, she thought it must be marvelous and secretly hoped that someday they would go there to live.

Margaret often sat looking wistfully up through the narrow basement windows at the blue sky, remembering her mama's smile, laughing with her two sisters, chasing her little brother, and sitting on her father's lap. She missed her family and home so much. But there was nothing she could do. She could never earn enough money to pay the train fare to Boston, no matter how hard she worked. And when she remembered her father's hurt, angry expression when she left, she knew there was little hope of ever seeing her family again.

One day the landlady of the house knocked on the basement door. Anna ran to answer, and the lady handed her a letter. Margaret knew immediately that the broadly scrawled handwriting on the envelope was her father's. With trembling fingers she pulled open the flap of the envelope. When she pulled out the single-sheet letter, two one-hundred dollar bills fell out on the floor. The letter had just three words: *"Please come home."*

———

Retold from public records

Come Home

$\mathcal{P}$lease come home." Are there any more wonderful words in the world? It is my personal hope and prayer that one of these stories may have touched your heart and brought you closer to home—home to your family, home to your friends, home to the God who loves you.

God's invitation of grace and love is always available. The door is open. The Father stands looking down the road, hoping to see you running toward him, waiting with his arms extended to gather you into his loving embrace, to welcome you home for eternity.

It's up to you to take the first step toward home, toward him. And he will run to meet you. Won't you answer with your contrite heart? He will hear, and he will forgive. Reach out in faith and obedience as you whisper his precious name:

Lord, I'm coming home.

———

Mary Hollingsworth

Bibliography

Allmon, India M. "The Teacher's Challenge." Used by permission of the author.

"Because of You." Written with facts in the public record.

Braden, Bernard. "Who's Listening?" Used by permission.

Bush, Barbara. "The Trouble with Cleaning." From the public record.

Chambers, Toni. "Still Singing." Used with permission.

Cherkofsky, Naomi. "Grandmother's Button Jar." *Woman's Day Magazine*, 1981.

Colson, Sidney. "What Would Jesus Do?" Used by permission.

Dobson, James. *Parenting Isn't for Cowards*. Nashville: Word Publishing, 1999. All rights reserved.

Dorsey, Tommy. "Precious Lord." New York: *Guideposts Magazine*. All rights reserved.

"God's Wings." Retold from facts in the public record.

Gordon, Arthur. *A Touch of Wonder*. Michigan: Baker Book House, 1982. All rights reserved.

Graham, Billy. *Unto the Hills*. Nashville: Word Publishing, 1996. All rights reserved.

Harvey, Paul. "Fathers."

Herrman, Dorothy. "Missed Charity."

Hollingsworth, Mary. *A Few Hallelujahs for Your Ho Hums*. Fort Worth: Brownlow, 1988. Used by permission of Shady Oaks Studio, Bedford, Tex.

_____. *Just Between Friends*. Fort Worth: Brownlow, 1987. Used by permission.

_____. "If Only." *On Raising Children*. Dallas: Word Publishing, 1993. Used by permission.

Keller, Helen. *The Story of My Life*. 1905.

Krohn, Rabbi Paysach. "God's Perfection." Used by permission.

"The Letter." Written with facts in the public record.

"Lights Out." Retold from facts in the public record.

"A Little Push." Written with facts in the public record.

Luther, Martin. "Confidence." Public domain.

Marshall, Arthur. "Seven-Year-Old Beauty."

Nelson, H. Lee. "Seeing Out." Used by permission of the author.

O'Leary, Denyse. "Waiting to be Asked." Used by permission of the author.

Powell, John. "Tommy." Used by permission.

Reece, Colleen L. "The Legacy." Used by permission.

Rees, Nigel. *The Cassell Dictionary of Anecdotes*. London: Cassell Wellington House, 1999.

_____. *Quote . . . Unquote.* London: Cassell Wellington House. 1980.

Reid, Rob. "The Tablecloth." Used by permission.

Roseveare, Helen. "Before You Ask." From a speech given by author, in the public record.

Sandburg, Carl. "Homecoming." Used by permission.

Scott, Darrell. "A Father's Plea." Public record.

Strong, Paschall N. "Terror of Buccaneer Bay." Used by permission.

Swindoll, Charles R. *Elijah: A Man of Heroism and Humility.* Nashville: Word Publishing, 2000. All rights reserved.

Thwaite, Ann. "You Don't Know Me, But. . ."

Tubman, Harriet. "'Twarnt Me." Public domain.

"The Waving Girl." Written with facts in the public record.

Williams, Margery. *The Velveteen Rabbit.* Public domain.

Worldwide Church of God. "The Hand."

Young, M. Norvel "Hang On, Brother!" Used by permission of Helen M. Young.

Zarandona, Josh and Karen. "The Ant and the Contact Lens." Used by permission.

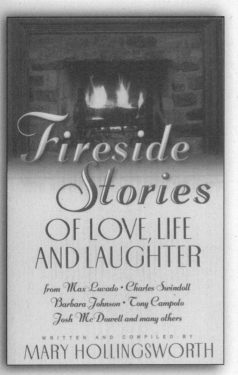